D1732861

THRASHIN' TIME

Illustrations by Jody Primoff

Thrashin' Time

Memories of a Montana Boyhood

By Milton Shatraw

AMERICAN WEST PUBLISHING COMPANY

PALO ALTO/CALIFORNIA

With appreciation and love
for my wife, Harriet
whose help, encouragement,
and unerring good judgment
made this book possible.

Contents

Introduction:
How It Happened

THE NORTHERN PACIFIC TRAIN rolled up the Yellowstone valley, crawled over the "hump," and continued along the newly born Missouri River until it finally stopped at the big ornate station at Helena. The hot summer afternoon air, heavy with smoke and cinders from the laboring engine, washed through the coach, but the seventeen-year-old boy staring out the open window never noticed it. He was too intent on absorbing everything in sight—from the rugged wooded mountains that half-circled the city to the wide golden sweep of the prairie as it reached out across the Prickly Pear valley to the high blue mountains in the hazy distance. He didn't even notice at first that the train had stopped and that people were getting off.

The year was 1887 and the boy was my father, Edward Shatraw, arriving from his farm home in northern New York state and about to start a brand new life in Montana. For the next thirty years he was to remain in the West, working at many jobs and in many places, but most of the time "ranching it" with his family on the prairieland just east of the high peaks of the Continental Divide, which the Indians called the "Shining Mountains."

He lived for a time in Helena with an older sister, Josie, and her husband, Alex Duval, who was head sawyer for the A. M. Holter Company, a prominent lumbering firm, but he soon decided to strike out on his own.

For several years he worked at a variety of jobs—ranch

1

hand, bartender, logger. He even tried working in Tommy
Cruze's big gold mine at Marysville. But an accident in which
he narrowly escaped death convinced him that this kind of work
belonged to the "cousin Jacks," as the Welsh miners were
called.

Sometime in the early 1890s my Uncle Alex bought a ranch
near Wolf Creek, a small town forty miles north of Helena, and
operated a sawmill in the mountains nearby. My father went to
work for him and soon after bought an adjoining ranch, where
he "batched it" for several years. About that same time he
bought a large twelve-horse, sweep-powered threshing machine,
which he and George Johnson, a young neighboring rancher,
operated every fall, doing the "thrashin'" for the ranchers in
the area. Somehow he still found time to attend every dance
and "spark" all the girls for miles around.

My mother's father, Joe Paice, a peppery little cockney
from London, arrived in Helena about the same time as my father did. He was a gardener and a good one, and he did very
well financially by landscaping the grounds around the beautiful homes being built in that prosperous city. In 1890 he returned to England and brought back his fifteen-year-old daughter, Emma, to keep house for him. She lived in Helena with
him and a younger sister, Annie (who had followed them from
London two years later), until the summer of 1898, when she
went to visit a family who owned a ranch near the Duvals at
Wolf Creek. Although she didn't particularly care for country
life, she decided to stay for the summer, working at the nearby
Gibson place. She had met my father by then, and I'm sure this
helped her to reach that decision.

My mother was small, red-headed, fiery, and considered
beautiful. My father was medium-sized, had coal-black hair and
dark blue eyes, and sported a racy red mustache. They fell in
love at first sight and were married that fall on Thanksgiving
Day. I always thought this a good omen, for theirs was a particularly happy marriage that lasted until my mother's death fifty
years later.

In the year following my parents' marriage, three important things happened: my older sister, Iris, was born; my father

renamed my mother Peggy, a name that stayed with her the rest of her life; and she filed on a one-hundred-sixty-acre homestead adjacent to our ranch. In order to prove up on this homestead, my father fenced the land and built a two-room log house, where they lived during the summers to establish their claim. I was born there on a hot July afternoon in 1901, and two years later my second sister, Lucy, arrived on the scene.

Sometime in 1905 my father sold our Wolf Creek ranches and entered into a partnership with another sister and her husband, my Aunt Minnie and Uncle George Therrien. They bought a ranch near the town of Dupuyer in Teton County, where we lived for two years at which time the partnership was ended, and we bought our own place nearby. The ranch was a mile square, with plenty of open rangeland stretching off to the north and south. The prairie was sprinkled with small ranches like ours, usually strung along the creeks that were born in the melting snows of the high Rockies to the west. Our new place was just south of the Blackfoot Indian reservation in the shadow of the Lewis Upthrust, that long line of jagged mountains that forms the Continental Divide and the eastern boundary of Glacier National Park.

My father and I loved this beautiful land. Here he built a brand new ranch; here he raised cattle and sheep, bred horses, and planted grain; and here my three brothers, Pat, Joe, and Harvey, were born. But my mother hated the loneliness of the long winters and feared the dangers of the untamed country. She deplored the lack of good schools, comfortable houses, adequate medical care, and future opportunities for her children. This was a serious disagreement between her and my father for many years.

The coming of the dry-land farmers, who took over the open range, fenced it, and plowed up the thin sod of the buffalo grass, ended ranching as my father knew it. About that time my mother had a serious operation and returned from the hospital far from well; as a result, when the opportunity came, we sold out and moved to Helena, where we lived for the next six years.

In 1918, after thirty-one years in Montana, my father returned to New York state and bought a large dairy farm high on the shoulder of a mountain in the western Catskills, near the town of Roxbury. It was a beautiful place, and we soon settled in among our neighbors and made many lasting friendships. But my father was never quite satisfied and still had the West in his blood. After a disastrous barn fire in 1924, he decided to return to Montana and to ranching. My mother and three younger brothers accompanied him while my married sisters and I remained in the East.

At that time the West was in the grip of the long drought of the twenties and thirties, and the dry-land farmers were giving up and moving on, leaving waste and desolation behind them. After some months of traveling around and talking to old friends, my father became convinced that the land had been ruined and would in time become a desert. Therefore, he returned again to his native state, where he worked for many years on a large estate near New York City. Although our family remained in the East, he never got over the feeling of loss and depression that followed that last visit to Montana.

"You know," he told me after he had come back, "when I first went into Teton County, I could ride horseback all day with the buffalo grass and wild hay brushing my stirrups. The streams ran full, and cattle grazed everywhere. But the drought and dry-land farming has changed everything. Now you see farm machinery abandoned in the fields. The houses are deserted, the people gone. The thin topsoil has blown away, leaving the land empty and bare, and everywhere the everlasting tumbleweed rolling across the fields, banking up against the rotting buildings, and caught in the tangled barbed wire fences. It's like the end of the world. I never want to go back."

My father never did go back, and neither did I until long after his death. I wish he might have been with me and Steve, my thirteen-year-old grandson, on a bright summer afternoon in 1967 when we drove along the bench and down into Sheep Creek valley and found his predictions wrong. After fifty-five years I found the house almost as we had left it, with the exception of a missing porch and the addition of a television antenna to the roof and a coat of brown stain. The bunkhouse was still standing next to the creek. It too had acquired a coat of brown stain, and a tall power pole stood in the wagonyard. There were horses in the barn and cattle in the pastures. There was no open range, and the fences were farther apart because the many small ranches had become a few huge ones, often consisting of thousands of acres. Normal rainfall and new planting methods had restored the pasture grasses and covered the prairie with productive strip-planted grainfields.

I found that most of the people we had known were gone, along with the houses they had so laboriously built. Some of our friends who stayed with the land had prospered, and some of my cousins were successful ranchers near Valier and Cutbank, with another one a stockman at Wolf Creek. I think of them all with affection and have only happy memories of my life among them.

These recollections of a man who was born and lived "out West" well over sixty years ago may vary in detail from the remembrances of other people who shared that experience. They are not meant to be a family history but rather—against a background of sparkling streams, wide, beckoning prairies and towering hazy blue mountains—a picture of life as he found it at that time and place.

MILTON SHATRAW
Roxbury, New York, 1970

Visiting Around

As far back as I can remember, I almost always went along with my father when he visited the neighbors or went into town. I was the oldest boy, with sisters who stayed home with my mother and brothers too young to go along. My father seemed to like to have me with him. Not that we talked very much, but we did have companionable silences. I also tried to be hanging around with wide open ears when people came to visit the ranch. So although we lived "forty miles from nowhere," as my London-born mother disgustedly located our Wolf Creek ranch, I did see quite a few people and got to know some of them quite well.

Many of these visits came about because my father had to arrange his threshing schedule for the coming fall during the summer months. He covered most of the ranches in a forty-mile circle, and that meant a lot of traveling for him and a lot of visiting for me. Another side occupation of my father's that required traveling about was horse breeding. Usually the mares were brought to our place, but sometimes my father took the stallion, tied to the back of our spring wagon, to the neighboring ranches; and I often went along.

One of his regular stops to arrange a threshing stand was at Sam Bissette's ranch. Sam was a wiry little Frenchman, with a scrubby grey mustache and excitable looking hair, who always made it clear to everyone that he was "boss of the ranch."

One day my father and I stopped at their place. It had been raining—one of our cold, early June rains—and as soon as we got in the house, Mrs. Bissette removed my soggy coat and shoes, and sat me in the rocking chair in front of the open oven door to dry out. I liked to go to Mrs. Bissette's because she was such a wonderful cook. She was a motherly woman, quiet and serene, who treated Sam and his noisy ways as if he were a rambunctious little boy. Her son, Arthur, was grown up, and she enjoyed mothering me, I'm sure, much as she had him twenty years earlier. Almost before I knew it, I had a thick slice of fresh-baked bread plastered with jam in one hand and a slab of chocolate layer cake in the other. Not being able to decide which to eat first, I tried alternating them, and that worked fine.

After settling the threshing date with my father, Sam took him down to the horse stable to pass judgment on a new team he had recently bought, leaving me in the kitchen while Mrs. Bissette went on with her work. Like most housewives in Rock Creek Basin, she scrubbed her floors on Fridays regardless of the weather. That day being Friday, she set briskly to work, slopping the water generously on the floor and shoving the chairs and table around, not missing even one small spot. She had just finished when my father and Sam, their boots filthy with mud, reached the back porch.

"Sam," Mrs. Bissette called out. "I've just mopped the floor; be sure to clean your boots good."

Sam glared at the half-open door for a minute, then stomped up the porch steps and tramped into the sparkling clean kitchen and back out again where he picked up the broom and began industriously to clean his boots.

We all watched him with open-mouthed amazement. Finally my father recovered his voice and demanded, "What the hell did you do that for, Sam?"

Sam went on brushing until the last gob of mud was off his boots. Then after staring defiantly toward his glowering wife, he turned to my father and said plaintively, "Damn it all, Ed, there's times when a man's just got to show his a't'ority!" Sam always had trouble with his English when he got a little excited.

Of course, I also went visiting with my mother at times, and some very interesting and exciting things occurred on these trips. She was a poor driver at best and inclined to panic when anything unusual happened. If a sudden blizzard or thunderstorm struck, she simply turned the whole matter of getting home over to the horse while we huddled under the blankets. She always carried a large cotton umbrella but used it only if the sun was out. If a thunderstorm appeared on the horizon, she immediately hid it under the seat, and we all got soaked. Lightning had once hit an umbrella she was holding, and though everyone assured her that lightning never strikes twice in the same place, she was determined not to give it a second chance.

Once in a while old Bugeater, this "safe" driving horse of my mother's, would show his contempt for her driving ability and for my father's trust in his reliability by backing up when he was supposed to go ahead. He could get up considerable speed too before ramming the buggy into a corral fence or log building. After he had proved his point, he usually sobered down and trotted us around the countryside with consideration and care.

The roads were in poor shape even in the best of weather, and to make matters worse, they were barred in dozens of places with gates. Our early Montana gates were often no better than the roads they crossed. They usually consisted of four strands of barbed wire nailed to one gatepost, the other ends fastened to a short pole, which had to be hooked into wire loops on the opposite post. It took considerable strength to operate one of these unwieldly things, and before I was old enough to handle them myself, I became familiar with some of my mother's favorite cusswords while helping her with the struggle. Opening a gate

wasn't the worst part. You drove up to the thing and got out and
the horse stayed put because he couldn't go anywhere until it was
opened. *Closing* it was another matter. First, he was led through
the gate, but then there was a lot of empty road ahead and no
one to hold the lines. My mother was faced with two choices:
she could turn the horse across the lane and up against the
fence, looping a line around a fencepost to be sure he stayed
there, or if she was in a gambling mood, she could wrap the
lines around the whip and take a chance that Bugeater would
wait until the gate was closed. My mother, a born gambler, always took the chance and usually won. Once in a while, though,
old Bugeater would get tired of waiting while she struggled
with the tangled gate and would suddenly decide to trot on
down the road without her. On hearing the clink of the iron-
rimmed wheels against the stones, my mother would scream out
an agonized "Whoa, Bugeater," drop the snarled-up barbed
wire, haul her skirts well above her knees, and take off after us.
Iris and I would kneel on the seat, facing backwards, and watch
with fascinated interest as she rapidly overtook the buggy and
clambered in over the back skinning her knees and losing her
hat in the process. Then breathing fire and brimstone, she
would reach over, grab the lines, and turn the old horse against
the nearby fence. Then she would walk wearily back to close
the gate, retrieving her hat on the way.

In spite of these little mishaps, my mother was always on
the lookout for an excuse to break up a lonesome afternoon
with a call on Aunt Josie or Mammy Johnson.

My father's sister, Aunt Josie, and Uncle Alex lived in a
big frame house—one of the few around—on the other side of a
hill to the south of us. My uncle had operated a sawmill at the
head of Wolf Creek and had ready access to real lumber instead
of the logs which most ranchers used. My aunt and uncle were
much older than my parents; as a result their family, with the
exception of two young daughters, were grown up or gone from
home. Flora, a husky tomboy, and Bessie, a dainty girl with long
golden curls, were always fun to be with.

Aunt Josie had "adopted" my mother when she arrived at
my father's homestead, a lost and bewildered city girl, and it

was to her that my mother turned when disaster struck. Aunt Josie had lived for years on a lonesome ranch and had raised a large family of children into healthy adults; she was well equipped to fight off sickness and death with her store of old family remedies that had come down through many generations of grandmothers. She once successfully doctored my older sister, Iris, through a desperate siege of scarlet fever, one of the early child killers.

Every year I had several bouts of croup, as most kids did in those good old days. I heard the story many times of how my mother frantically summoned her sister-in-law one winter afternoon when I was two years old and was in bed with a very bad attack of this scary disease. Aunt Josie jumped from the buggy before it had really stopped and hurried through the back door to the crib standing beside the kitchen stove. After a quick look at my blue face and labored breathing, she turned to my mother and gasped, "My God, Peggy! He's dying!"

My mother, already frightened half out of her wits, turned on her in fury. "If that's all the help you can be, Josie Duval, you can get out of here and leave us alone." Then she burst into tears.

That did it. Aunt Josie stripped off her coat and hat and took charge. "Don't worry, Peg," she promised. "I'll have him well in no time."

She turned to my father, who had tied the team to the fence and hurried in to help. "Get that fire going good, Eddy, and put plenty of water on to boil. We've got to have lots of steam. And I'll need some turpentine and sugar."

They half drowned me in steam and fed me small balls of butter that had been rolled in sugar and topped off with a drop of turpentine—an old French remedy, she said. But what I liked best, they told me later, was the cough medicine Aunt Josie concocted by diluting honey with a little whisky. I guess I was pretty well loaded by midnight, but I was also feeling fine and slept it off the next day, the first good sleep in a week.

Medical help was not the best and very hard to get in any case; most of the ranch people had to depend on themselves or one another in emergencies. Some became expert in certain things. With Aunt Josie it was croup. They all had favorite remedies which they relied on, but the one universal remedy they all stuck with was whisky.

Whisky was, of course, the recognized cure for snake bite, and I heard about a few men who dosed themselves liberally when threatened with a foot-long garter snake. Once while we were building our new house, my cousin Frank chopped his foot badly with an ax. My father bandaged it with strips cut from an old grainsack and gave him a teacupful of whisky from the bottle kept in the toolshed for just such emergencies. He was back at work within a week. Whisky was used to cure colds, chills and fever, and "summer complaint." One of our hired men who was bald as an egg doused his scalp regularly with Old Crow, thoroughly convinced that he would one day grow hair. Even the women used it for special cures. I once heard Mrs. Howe telling my mother that she always had some brandy on hand in case she had a miscarriage. Miscarriage was a strange disease to me, and I couldn't remember anyone ever having had it, but I hoped mother would be prepared, as Mrs. Howe suggested, in case I ever came down with it.

Many of the ranchers who depended on hard liquor for doctoring their families also used it to dose sick cows and horses. It didn't usually help the suffering animals much, but a bottle in the house was a godsend to the homesteader as he sweated out a long night acting as midwife to his favorite mare. But whisky could sometimes effect very dramatic cures on animals too, as Ebenezer Johnson proved to my father and me one cold winter afternoon.

We had gone to the sawmill with supplies for the crew that were getting out logs and stockpiling them for the next cut. Dinner with the logging crew had been fun, and now we were on our way back, ghosting along behind a frisky team, warm and comfortable under the horse blankets that covered the straw-filled sleighbox. We caught up with Eb as he was riding toward his ranch with a young calf across his saddle. It was a miserable day with a stiff north wind driving the snow in a long slant across the prairie, and both Eb and the calf looked half frozen. As we pulled alongside, my father surveyed the situation and called out, "Need any help, Eb?"

"Gotta' get this critter under cover and warmed up or he's a goner," Eb shouted back.

We stopped, and the two men put the little white-faced calf into the sleigh and covered him with a blanket. His legs were stiff, and he shuddered convulsively. I looked at his soaked hair and rolled back eyes, and I too figured he was a "goner." A short time later we stopped in front of the Johnson's house, where Ed dismounted and picked up the calf. "Put the horses in the cow shed for now," he called over his shoulder. "We'll take care of them later."

By the time my father and I reached the kitchen, Eb and his wife had the calf on a blanket in front of the red-hot stove. We all stood around the poor little thing wondering what to do.

"What he needs," my father suggested, "is something hot inside him."

Eb's eyes lit up, and he turned to his wife. "You got thum Jamaica ginger, Lib?" Eb had a strong lisp, and when he said "thum" I wanted to laugh, but a look from my father changed my mind.

Lib started for the pantry, "Bring a pan, too," he ordered, as he reached down a bottle of whisky from the shelf behind the stove.

He poured a full pint of whisky into the pan, dissolved a heaping spoonful of ginger in it, and put it on the stove to heat. Two minutes later he tasted it, shook his head, and added some more ginger. Still not enough! He looked at his wife and asked, "You got thum cayenne pepper, Lib?"

She hurried off, returning in a minute with a large tin of the fiery stuff. Eb added a generous spoonful to the "medicine" and stirred vigorously.

"You'll kill that calf, Eb," my father warned.

But Eb shook his head. "I'd better try it and thee if it'th hot enough," and he took a healthy swig from the pan.

At first he acted as if he had had a stroke, standing stiff as a statue. Then he carefully set the pan down and clutched his throat with both hands, moaning softly to himself. Finally, he drew a long, shuddering breath and gasped, "Jumping Jehosaphat!" and made for the water pail. After drinking two dippers of water and wiping his eyes with a dirty bandanna, he passed judgment on the mixture.

"Just right," he said and stepped over to pick up an empty bottle that lay in the corner. Lib wasn't much of a housekeeper.

The calf, in the meantime, hadn't shown much sign of life. It was just lying stiffly on the blanket, shivering and gasping for breath. Eb filled the bottle with his hot drink and, kneeling down, took the calf's head tenderly in the crook of his arm, then slipped the neck of the bottle into the calf's mouth and poured the liquid down its throat.

At first the calf froze just as Eb had done, then with a strangled bleat it lunged to its feet, knocking Eb sprawling, and tore wildly around the kitchen, upsetting chairs and breaking a leg off the table.

We finally got him corralled and quieted down, and an hour later, when we left, he had drunk a couple quarts of warm milk and was well on the road to recovery.

When I crawled into the bobsled to start the trip home, the short winter afternoon was almost gone. It was still snowing some, and the north wind had a bite that promised a mighty cold night, but I was warm and glowing all the way home from the excitement.

Dad Johnson, Eb's brother and one of the first white settlers in the area, lived with his wife, Susan, and his only child, George, in a rambling dirt-roofed house on the other side of our shallow valley. We all called them Dad and Mammy Johnson because my father did. George and my father were close friends, who had threshed and logged and fenced and broken wild horses together for so many years that they seemed to be one family.

This old couple, though probably only in their late fifties, seemed to me to be about a hundred years old. Mrs. Johnson never seemed to work much, at least when I was around, but sat in a well-padded rocking chair beside the window that looked out over the valley and the county road that ran between Wolf Creek and Augusta. A crank telephone was screwed to the wall above her head, its receiver hanging by a cord tied to a hook and dangling within inches of her ear. With her eyes on the road and her ear to the telephone, she knew everything that happened in Rock Creek Basin and was the center of information for my mother and Aunt Josie and all the other women who couldn't afford this modern gadget or didn't have the time to listen to it.

Dad Johnson didn't seem to work much either but just followed the shade around the house in the summer and kept close to the fire in winter. Like all the other old-timers, he was a great teller of tales, some of which were true but most of which were exaggerations or just plain "lies," as Mammy called them. He was always on the lookout for an audience, and I spent a lot of cold afternoons perched on the woodbox listening while he did his remembering and smoked his pipe in the nearby armchair. In the summer we were usually outdoors in some shady spot.

"Yes sir," he said to me one sunny afternoon after we had made ourselves comfortable on the wide stone step. "It was a day just like this when I had my last ruckus with those murdering Blackfoot Indians."

Dad Johnson's Indian stories were his very best ones, and it was hard to wait while he stoked up his pipe, got it lit and drawing properly, and then went on. "I was sitting right here like I am now when this squaw came around the corner of the house and nearly rode right over me. She must have come down from the hills out back and been pretty quiet about it, 'cause I hadn't heard a thing. She had an old-time buffalo gun across the saddle horn, pointing right at me, and one of Mammy's best Buff Orpington hens tied to the saddle.

" 'Hold it!' I yelled. 'Where you going in such an all-fired hurry? And that's my chicken you got there.'

"She stopped but didn't say anything, just sat on her horse and looked at me. She was a young, good-looking squaw, at least as near as I could tell under a big black hat and all those clothes they always wear.

"I pointed at the hen. 'Give it to me!' I said.

" 'No!' she said. 'I caught him. He's mine;' and she raised the gun a little.

"I was gettin' mad by that time and jumped up, yelling for her to give me the gun and reaching for it. Just then the damn thing went off.

"Well! There was so much smoke and noise, I couldn't hear for a minute, but I knew I'd got hit all right. Finally I made her out, hightailing it off across that alfalfa field, only it wasn't alfalfa then, just flat prairie, and I was sitting down here holding onto my legs.

"Yes sir," he went on, "shot me in both shins. There—see!" and he pulled up his faded overalls. All I could see was some long grey underdrawers stuffed into blue hand-knit wool socks. But I was impressed all the same.

"Gee," I said. "That must have hurt."

"Naw!" he bragged. "Not much. The gun was loaded with rusty nails and chunks of wire and stuff like that, and the powder must have been damp 'cause it didn't have much kick, so all it did was tear up my pants and knock some skin loose."

He sat for a minute looking at his skinny shanks and thinking about it, I guess, for he added sadly, "But she sure raised hell with a damn good pair of boots."

That night at supper I told how old Mr. Johnson had got shot in the legs by a pretty Indian girl. My father laughed, but my mother looked grim.

"Ed," she asked, "do you think that old man ought to be telling little kids like Mick such awful lies?"

But my father just shrugged his shoulders "I don't know. Old Dad Johnson had a lot to do with settling Rock Creek Basin," he said thoughtfully, "and, now he's an old man, and George has taken over. I suppose he feels left out of things and talks a lot about the past to make up for it. Maybe he does exaggerate, even lie a little. But I don't see as he does any harm." He looked at me. "How about it, Mick? You like to listen to his stories, don't you?"

"You bet!" I said. "But the Indian ones are best."

When I was about five years old, my father began talking about moving north a hundred miles to a different ranch near Dupuyer, a small town in Teton County. "Rock Creek Basin," he explained to my mother, "is getting too crowded. I like to see miles of open rangeland around me, so I can have a little room to breathe."

My mother thought it a step backward but didn't complain too much, even though the railroad would be forty miles away instead of ten, and we hardly knew a soul up there. She realized it was my father's kind of country and understood how he felt about it, even though she dreaded the unknown dangers she was sure were lurking up there and the long lonesome weeks when he would be away with the threshing rig.

But it sounded beautiful to me, like one long, wonderful visit, with a lot of different people to see and a million new and exciting things to do.

So my father and his brother-in-law, Uncle George, became partners and bought a ranch up there. It was actually two ranches rolled into one, and we would live on one while Aunt Minnie and Uncle George lived on the other.

We left for our new home in midsummer. It was a two-day drive with horses, and we needed an early start in order to reach the Beaupré Hotel in Choteau, our half-way point, by dark. But since my mother insisted on supervising the loading of the wagon that would follow with all our belongings, it was late in the morning by the time she settled herself in the buggy, the baby in her arms, and my father beside her. Iris and I sat on folding stools at their feet, and we didn't see much during the trip because the horses' backsides were directly in front of us, and our parents towered over us from behind. We rolled steadily along the rough road but were still some miles short of Choteau at sundown. The rugged mountains of the Basin had given way to rolling prairie on every side, and by now we could make out the long blue line of the high mountains far to the west.

My father pointed with his whip. "See that V in the mountains, just to the left of where the sun set?" he asked. "Well, that's where Sheep Creek starts. Our place is five or six miles downstream, and it's a beautiful place—rangeland north and south as far as you can see and plenty of room for meadows and grainfields in the valley. We got good water rights and good land, and ought to make some real money up there."

My mother was getting tired and answered with a bit of a

sniff in her tone. "Where's all those people that are getting rich around here? Haven't seen a house in the last two hours, and I don't see any now. Looks like a good place to raise coyotes and jackrabbits to me. And that looks like a storm coming up." She pointed to a black cloud that had suddenly appeared off to the northwest.

"Shucks," my father answered, "that's nothing. Probably blow by in a few minutes."

Half an hour later we were in the middle of the worst rain and lightning storm I'd ever seen. We arrived at the hotel, scared, discouraged, and soaking wet; but the kindly Beauprés dried us out, fed us, and bedded us down for the night. The next morning brought a sparkling new day.

We quickly settled down in our new house and were soon acquainted with our neighbors. My mother lost some of her distrust of the wild country, but she would gladly have traded the towering blue mountains I loved so well for a line of houses, and our clear-running Sheep Creek for a busy street.

My father was contented again, busy with plans to expand the ranch and driving around arranging his threshing schedule. He had always bred horses, and now in this more open country he could do even more along this line.

Sometimes it seemed to me that he loved his horses almost as much as he did his family. He petted and fondled the colts until they became so gentle that there was no trouble when it came time to break them to harness. He hated to sell a team, fearing they might be mistreated by their new owner. For a time he sold teams to the U.S. government to be used on the Panama Canal project but quit when he learned that a northern horse lived but a few months in that climate.

After supper on summer evenings, when the workhorses had finished their allowance of oats, I would help my father lead them across the plank bridge over the creek and down the lane to the pasture. There he would slip their halters free and drive them through the gate with a friendly slap on the rump. Afterward he would stand leaning on the polegate, an amused smile on his face, while the horses went through the ritual of the evening roll. After sniffing out just the right place, they would clumsily lie down and struggle to roll completely over. It took a lot of snorting and groaning, but they finally made it. Then, heaving themselves to their feet, they shook the dust from their glossy summer coats and wandered off into the twilight, munching tender buffalo grass as they went.

It was the quiet time of the day with nothing to hear but the muffled footfalls of a grazing horse, or the distant bawling of a range cow looking for a misplaced calf, or sometimes a pair of coyotes tuning up on the flank of Scoffin Butte. I knew that coyotes were cowards, but even so there was something scary about their wild howling at night, and I would keep close beside my father as we walked through the deepening gloom toward the yellow glow of the kitchen lamplight.

Soon after we came to Dupuyer, my father and some of the neighbors, in order to improve the quality of their stock, formed a horse breeding company and bought a Belgian stallion who weighed over a ton. He was kept at our place in a big ten-foot-high corral down along the creek, and no one handled him except my father or one of the more experienced hired men. Usually the mares were brought to our ranch, and Nero, as he was called, performed his chores down behind the barn with ear-splitting squeals and snorts and considerable tearing up of the ground. But sometimes my father had to take Nero to a neighboring ranch, and since he was no cowboy but preferred the comfortable seat of a springwagon to a hard leather saddle, I could often go along and visit with the folks while Nero worked hard at increasing the horse population of Teton County.

Though I shared my father's fondness for horses, I was more apt, on those evenings when we took them down to the pasture, to be looking off at the jagged mountains, standing dark against the afterglow. The mountains fascinated me, and I was always wondering what was on the other side of them.

My cousin Leo had told me about the high Mission Mountains and Flathead Lake, which was so long you couldn't see from one end to the other. I had always wanted to see a real lake and was forever asking about it when he came over to help with the ranch work.

Because we lived on the same ranch with Uncle George

and Aunt Minnie, their barely grown sons, Leo and Frank, did
a lot of running back and forth helping with the work, and
both families did a lot of visiting. We doubled up to do most of
the heavy ranch work such as haying, threshing, working cattle,
and repairing fences and buildings. There was one thing we always did together that caused a lot of excitement and that I
could never see any reason for. Uncle George would drive up
without warning one day and have all my little cousins with
him but not Aunt Minnie. They would stay all night, and we
would have a grand time. Next day Uncle George would reap-
pear and proudly announce that there was a new baby at his
house. Occasionally it was the other way around, and all of us
kids would have a hurried overnight visit with Aunt Minnie and
return next day to find out *we* had a new baby brother. These
new arrivals always astonished me, but no one else seemed to be
too surprised.

Overnight visits with my cousins were a lot of fun, especially when I was the visitor. My aunt was ordinarily a gentle,
easygoing person like my father, but sometimes the kids riled
her to a point where she blew up. Her recriminations started
out in English but at the end usually slid into the more familiar
and expressive French of her girlhood. I listened in awe one day
while she dressed down my cousin Joe, marveling at the easy
flow of her scolding and the bloodcurdling threats she promised
him, until finally her English failed her and she stuttered to a
frustrated halt, paused a moment, then finished triumphantly,
"You . . . you *petit face de coq!*"

I wondered what she had called him and made sure to find
out, thinking they were some special kind of French cusswords.
When I asked Joe later what she had said, he laughed. "Heck,"
he said, "she just called me a 'little rooster-face.' "

But her husband, Uncle George, was by far the most excitable person I knew and could get the maddest, especially if the
joke was on him. One summer an ornery range cow hung
around the buildings, and no amount of driving her away was
successful. Sooner or later she would be back, hunting for an un-
latched gate or an unlocked barn door and threatening everyone within sight with her long, sharp horns.

My mother had spent an hour up in the garden one morning, weeding and hoeing, and was on her way back to the house with a bundle of bright red rhubarb stalks under one arm and a pail of freshly picked peas dangling from the other. This cross-grained old cow must have been biding her time, for when all the fences were well beyond my mother's reach, she came tearing down the path snorting death and destruction. My mother was no heroine as far as the ranch animals were concerned; she dropped the rhubarb and peas, gathered up her skirts and lit out for the house. She beat the old cow through the kitchen door by inches and slammed it shut but was still stewing under high pressure when my father came in at noon from mowing the north meadow. Within minutes he was unconditionally agreeing that the only thing that cow was good for was corned beef and the sooner the better for everyone. Since he was always a little squeamish about killing things, Uncle George agreed to come down that evening to act as executioner and help with the butchering that would follow.

The cow had been locked up in the corral that afternoon to provide some semblance of safety for us humans, and when we congregated down there after supper she was pacing around, spoiling for a fight. Uncle George checked his gun, rested it on a fence rail, took careful aim, and fired. The cow dropped and lay motionless in the dirt. My uncle flashed a triumphant grin from behind his handlebar mustache and climbed the fence, butcher knife in hand to finish her off. Apparently the bullet had only stunned her, for the prick of the knife as it slit her throat brought her up snorting and charging. Uncle George always claimed he was just startled by her actions, but it was plain to all of us by the way he tore across the corral and shot over the fence that he was scared half to death. Leo always claimed that Uncle George's feet never touched the ground as he crossed the corral and sailed over the fence like a feather in a cyclone. The cow, in the meantime, after a few faltering steps, collapsed and died.

He never quite forgave us for laughing at him, and it was always a touchy joke in the family. I remember hearing my mother twitting him one time about his fancy footwork that day and Uncle George yelling back at her that he "was *not* scared!" Words finally failed him, and he jerked off his hat, threw it on the floor, and jumped on it. With his feelings relieved, he picked up the hat, jammed it on his head, and stomped out of the house.

A year or so later we bought the old Pete Bergland place and moved a mile farther up Sheep Creek to the new house my father had built. We didn't see quite so much of Uncle George and his family after that, and I missed them and all the excitement that seemed to follow them around.

One of the first things I discovered up there was the remains of a log house across the road where someone had lived long ago. I used to sneak over and lie on my stomach on the rotting boards that partly covered the old well, staring at the clear water far below and hollering down it to hear the echo. My mother was sure I'd fall in if I fooled around there, and gave strict orders to stay away, which I promptly forgot. One of the things that puzzled me was why the stones that lined the well didn't come apart and the whole thing collapse. I asked my father about it and was told that it was the "one-over-two" method of laying stones.

"When you finish digging a well," he said, "and are ready to line it, you start with a ring of stones on the bottom, all about the same size. When the next layer goes on, each rock covers the joint of the two below it. You keep doing this as you lay each ring of stones, and when the top is reached, everything is locked together and the lining will stand for years."

My mother continued worrying about the well and tried to get my father to fill it in. "Someday one of the kids will fall in and drown. You've got to do something."

"That's the Alcorn place," my father argued, "one of the oldest settlers in Teton County. And I hear he's still around. I can't ruin his well, can I?"

My mother answered with a simple emphatic "*Yes!*" then added, "it's better than having one of the kids drowned, isn't it?"

So my father went over there one day with some pieces of plank and some twenty-penny spikes and built a solid cover

over it. I never did lie on my stomach again and hang my head way down so that my voice seemed to come from China when I hollered, or drop a stone in the water and hear the hollow *thunk* that sounded as if the water were a mile deep.

One afternoon I went down to Aunt Minnie's, and there was a very old man sitting in the rocker by the window. He had a long white beard and hair so thin I thought he was bald at first. He looked tired and sick, and didn't pay any attention to me. When we went outside, I asked Joe about him.

"Oh, that's old man Alcorn," he said. "He hasn't any family, and Ma's going to take care of him for a while. He's pretty sick."

"What's the matter with him?" I wondered.

Joe shrugged his shoulders carelessly, "Just old, I guess."

I went back one afternoon some time later to bring the mail that my cousin Lily had dropped off at our place on her way home from town. Aunt Minnie was pleased to get her mail but still more pleased to see me.

"Everybody is away except the little kids. I want to go see Mrs. Rappold (her nearest neighbor downstream) about a dress pattern and don't like to leave Mr. Alcorn alone. Will you stay with him until I get back? I'll only be gone a little while, and I'll take the kids along."

"I guess so," I said, " 'long as I get home by suppertime."

"I'll be back in plenty of time for that," she promised. "Mr. Alcorn's very sick now and has to stay in bed. You stay in the bedroom in case he needs anything." She pushed me into the room. "The boy here will stay with you till I get back from the Rappolds'," she told him. "Now don't try to get up. Just ask for anything you want."

The old man nodded, and my aunt hurried off leaving me standing in the doorway. We stared at one another for a few minutes, and I noticed his eyes were dark blue and sharp. They didn't look sick to me.

"Sit down," he said, looking at the chair by the window, and again I was surprised because his voice, though low and weak, was clear and easy to understand.

My aunt had put a kitchen chair at the head of the bed

with its back down and its legs stuck up in the air. With a pillow against it, it made a fine back rest.

"Can't lay down anymore; get all choked up," he explained. "Sure is hell to get old!"

We sat quietly for a while; then he asked, "What's your name and where do you live?"

"I'm Mick. We live on the old Bergland place," I answered.

"Yah. I heard somebody built a house up there, right across from my old cabin."

"I go over there a lot, and Pa covered up the old well. 'Fraid the little kids might fall in."

"That was a good well," the old man said. "Hate to see it filled in."

"Oh, Pa wouldn't do that. He said it belonged to you. He just nailed some planks over it."

Mr. Alcorn smiled. "Glad to hear that. That's a mighty fine well. Never went dry that I can remember. And it saved my life once, too!"

I sat quiet, holding my breath, because I was pretty sure there was a story coming up, and those old-timers could tell dandies.

Suddenly he held out his big-knuckled right fist and pulled up the sleeve of the heavy red undershirt, exposing a heavy-boned forearm covered with stringy muscle and withered skin.

"Thirty years ago I was as strong as a bull and a damn good thing, too, or I might not be here today. Didn't think I'd ever get old. Now look at that." He didn't sound sad or sorry for himself exactly, just kind of amazed that such a thing could happen to him.

He settled back and rested for a few minutes. "I was one of the first settlers around here and got along good with the Indians most of the time. No reservation then, but they didn't bother me none.

"Always liked that spot up there on Sheep Creek, so I built me a cabin there one summer. Just a squatter then. Took out papers later, though. And I dug me a well. Took a month to dig it and line it, and I packed in some plank and made a cover so nothing could fall in it and spoil the water. Best water I ever tasted. Yes, sir," he went on thoughtfully. "Best damn well I ever saw!

"I heard some talk that fall about the Blackfeet being kind of restless, so when I got up at daybreak one morning and saw a half-dozen painted bucks following along the creek, sneaking among the willows, I knew I was in for trouble. I was just getting ready to make a run for it, when I happened to think about the well.

"I slipped out the door, and by good luck the cabin hid me till I was in the well and the cover in place. I had nailed a crossbar on the underside of the lid and tied a rock to it so the wind couldn't blow it off. I got a good hold on the bar, braced my back and feet against the sides of the well, and waited.

"After a while I heard them banging around the house and figured they were stealing everything they could carry off. I only hoped they wouldn't burn the cabin. Finally an Indian came over and tried to lift the well cover. I gritted my teeth and hung on. The first Indian gave up and called for help; another one came to help him, and the two of them heaved on the handle. Lucky for me the handle pulled loose, and they went sprawling. They got up and talked it over in Indian, so I don't know what they said. But I guess they figured it was stuck and just wandered off.

"I stayed down in that well all day, and when it got dark I crawled out. They didn't burn the cabin, but it was clean as a whistle—stole everything I owned. I didn't hang around very long but lit out for Choteau as fast as I could lope. Came back the next summer when things had quieted down. Never ranched it up there very much though. Too busy hunting and trapping over in the big mountains."

He was kind of winded by then so we sat quiet and rested.

"Gosh," I said after a while, "I bet you were scared."

"Scared!" he chuckled and his eyes twinkled. "You know, Mick," he said, "two days later I cut my foot with the ax, and I didn't bleed a drop. Heart hadn't really got going again, I guess."

Mr. Alcorn died a short time later and hardly anyone went

to his funeral. People soon forgot about him, I suppose, but I never did, especially the twinkle in his eye and his amused chuckle when he told about his Indian scare.

The one thing I liked best about the stories that these old-timers like Mr. Alcorn and Dad Johnson told was the way they laughed at themselves. My father and Uncle Alex were like that, too, and the worse the scare, the louder the laugh. Like the time the safety valve stuck on the steam boiler up at the saw-mill, and it blew up with a bang that was heard for miles.

They were telling my grandfather about it the next time he visited us for a few days of trout fishing. "You know, Joe," Uncle Alex told him, "Ed here was in such a hurry to leave that engine shack that he never bothered to open the door, just ripped the hinges and lock off like they were made of paper."

"How did you know what I did?" my father retorted. "The last I saw of you, you were on a flying leap toward the sawdust pile and dove in like a bullfrog in a mill pond."

And they both leaned back in their chairs and roared.

My ginger-haired grandfather, London-born and without a speck of humor in his whole make-up, glared at them in disgust.

"What's the matter with them two damn fools?" he snorted to my mother. "Don't they know they might have been killed?"

It sounded funny to me, too, and I laughed; but I could see that my mother agreed with Grandpa. My father claimed that the best way to get over being half scared to death was to laugh about it. All the old-timers did anyway. And even Aunt Josie, who was always so kind and gentle, could laugh wholeheartedly at one of these near disasters once they were past. A few days before the afternoon when I almost suffocated with croup, we had visited her, and I had begged her to give me some of the bacon rinds she was trimming off a slab of bacon. Thinking they were not the best thing for me to chew on, she had firmly refused in spite of all my wheedling. But when she had nursed me that long night, thinking I might die, she prayed aloud to herself and added after each prayer, "Oh God! Why didn't I give him those bacon rinds?"

Later everyone, including Aunt Josie, laughed about the

ending of those fervent prayers; and from then on whenever she came hurrying to help us in some crisis, my father would relieve the tension by asking with a smile, "Josie, did you bring some bacon rinds?"

In times of trouble Aunt Josie never arrived with bacon rinds, of course, but she brought instead, as all our neighbors and relatives did, help, sympathy, and understanding, as well as a wonderful sense of humor. All these get-togethers for other than tragic reasons were my kind of visiting, and they hardly ever ended with a polite, "I had a lovely time" but instead with a shouted joke and an uninhibited laugh as the departing visitors turned toward home. It was our way of saying good-bye.

The House My Father Built

A BIG CALENDAR ALWAYS HUNG on the west wall of the ranch house kitchen. Under the picture in inch-high letters were the words, COMPLIMENTS OF HARRIS BROS., GENERAL MERCHANDISE, DUPUYER, MONTANA. This year it had an exciting picture of a big black pacer and his gaily dressed driver, with the simple title "Dan Patch" underneath.

Dan Patch, my father had explained to me, was the fastest harness racing horse in the world, never beaten in a fair race. But much as my father loved horses such as this black beauty, it was the back of the calendar that interested him most (and all the rest of us) that summer of 1907, when he planned the new ranch house he was going to build. The calendar being the only large piece of drawing paper he could lay his hands on, he would take it from its hook in the evening after the dishes were done, lay it face down on the kitchen table, place the green-shaded coal-oil lamp where he could get the best light, then start working out detailed plans for the new house while we all crowded around offering suggestions.

"It's going to be the best damn log house in Teton County," he would tell my mother proudly, and my father being a man of his word, she and all the rest of us believed him.

My father and Uncle George had found that their partnership ranch was too small for two families to own and operate together. Thus, when the old Bergland property—a mile upstream—came up for sale, my father decided to buy it. Uncle George and Aunt Minnie would stay at the old place, and next year, after the run-down fences and buildings of the new ranch were in shape, we would move up to our new home.

One day in early summer my father took mother up to inspect the new purchase. The buggy left the main road and followed the twin ruts that wandered a long half mile up the flank of Scoffin Butte, twisting among the buckbrush and dodging the swales and steeper grades. Pete Bergland, from whom my father had bought the ranch, was an "Old batch" and from the look of the buildings, it was easy to see he had lived in an offhand sort of way. There was a deserted-looking but sturdy one-room log house, a good-sized cattle shed built of poles covered with a flat brush-and-wild-hay roof, and a tumbledown log horse barn.

My mother coldly eyed first the layout, then my father.

"Well, Ed, if you think I'm going to live way up here off the road in this godforsaken hole, you've got another think coming."

"Hell, Peg, we could fix it up. I'll add an ell for a couple of bedrooms and—"

"And," my mother picked him up, "you'll live up here all by yourself. I'm not going to bury myself and the children . . ." and off she went on one of her laying-down-the-law speeches, complete with fist-pounding and foot-stomping.

My father waved his hands in surrender and finally got the torrent of words stopped.

"All right! All right! We'll build another house if that's the way you feel." Then he added with a twinkle in his eye, "I knew you wouldn't live up here, and neither would I, but it sure livens things up when you blow up. Anyway, I've got a jim-dandy place picked out for the new house, across the creek and right by the road. I'll build the barns on this side of the stream." He swung the team around and headed back for the site of the new ranch house at a bone-rattling trot, as they eagerly discussed plans for the building of their new home.

From the first, one of the toughest problems with the new house was the water supply. There was no gushing spring such as we had at our present house anywhere near the new site.

"We'll have to dig a well and get a pump for it," my father said.

But my mother shook her head. "I'm not going to like that one bit," she said. "I hate outdoor pumps and open wells. They're freezing up in the winter, and snakes and gophers falling in and drowning."

"What we need," my father said, "is one of those London water mains coming down the valley." (He liked to tease my mother for being a Londoner in the Wild West.)

She made a face at him, and the matter was dropped for the time being.

Along with the first mention of a new house came my mother's demand that it have a real parlor. My father was aghast. Waste all that space on a room that would be used only a couple of times a year?

"What we need, Peg," he argued at first as he worked on the plans, "are bedrooms, not a place for showing off fancy furniture. Maybe later."

But my mother was adamant. "I want a parlor now," she said fiercely. "All that beautiful furniture you won on that raffle ticket lying under tarps down in the granary all this while! When do you think I want to use them? On my golden wedding day?"

"Oh, all right," he grumbled. "How big has it got to be?"

"Let's see," she said happily; "the ticket said one sofa, one platform rocker, four walnut chairs, a marble-topped table, a bookcase, and two whatnots. I've never seen them," she added wistfully, "except peeking through the straw wrapping. But I glimpsed the carved walnut arms and the horsehair upholstery. They're so pretty, Ed. They've got to have a room of their own. One big enough to hold them, that's all."

My father groaned as he studied the trial plan he had started to draw.

"This long narrow house won't work then. It would be like

a railroad car—mostly aisle. And a square one wouldn't be any better. Too dark."

My cousin Frank spoke up, laughing. "I guess you'll have to build two houses, Uncle Ed. A long one and a square one. Be an awful lot of running back and forth though."

We all snickered, but my father didn't laugh. He scratched his head and stared at the paper. At last he said, "That's exactly what I'll do, only I'm going to fasten them together. The kitchen, pantry and maybe a bedroom in the long ell—the sitting room, bedrooms, *and parlor* in the square part."

And that's how the house got its shape.

It had been a good hay summer that year. By the middle of August the last big haystack was topped off, the mower and rake backed into the wagon shed, and the rope tackle coiled and stored in the loft above it. This last day had been a busy one, and we were all sitting outside the kitchen door in the early twilight. The talk switched back and forth between the new house and preparations for starting the fall threshing trip, now less than a month away.

"We'll have to have some sort of shed up there," my father said, "while we're working on the house this winter—to keep tools in and to get in out of the weather when it's bad."

"Too bad old Pete didn't build his cabin down by the creek," my mother said. "That would have been just the thing."

I was sitting in the grass by my father's chair, listening and feeling pretty much left out of all the planning. I felt I had to join in even at the risk of saying something dumb and being laughed at.

"Hey, Pa," I said. "I'll bet if you hitched old Mike and Jim onto that cabin, they could drag it down."

Everyone shouted with laughter, just as I feared. Everyone, that is, except my father, who suddenly reached over and ruffled my shock of unruly hair. "By God, Mick," he said. "I think you've got it!"

"Hell, Uncle Ed," my cousin Leo said. "You don't think those two horses could even budge that log cabin, let alone—"

"Of course not," my father interrupted. "But if we jacked it up and put about four skid logs underneath, then hitched about ten good teams to it, they could haul it down there, all right."

"You'd have to do some ducking around to keep it on the level," Nolan, the hired man, chipped in. "And watch out to miss that swampy spot. But it is all downgrade. Yessir! I'll bet we could do it."

A few days later, with the help of our neighbors and their teams and accompanied by clouds of prairie dust and the powerful smell of sweating horses and men, the first building for our new ranch settled into its place beside the clear-running water of Sheep Creek.

But the time was short until mid-September, when all the men on the ranch would leave with the threshing rig on its annual six-week tour. The next few weeks my father and the hired men worked from daylight till dark, selecting, cutting, and trimming the long straight pines and fir trees that grew on a shoulder of Split Mountain, hauling them down the rough woods road and dumping them on the growing log pile across the creek from the old cabin.

Hard work and good luck paid off because my father had the satisfaction of knowing that enough logs to build the new house lay ready at the building site before he left for his first threshing stand.

It was well into November when he and the rig returned on a cold, snowy afternoon. I followed my father around in a daze of happiness as he did the evening chores, asking countless questions about the threshing trip and relating my idea of the latest and most exciting news. It was wonderful to have him home. Everyone felt safe and comfortable again. Already the look of anxiety and worry that had lain on my mother's face these last few weeks had disappeared. Even the teacher came to the supper table in a freshly starched and ironed shirtwaist that night, and I think she felt in her heart some of the same love we all had for him.

True to our freaky Montana weather, the next Saturday morning was as fine as any in June. At breakfast my father announced that it would be a great day to stake out the exact piece of ground that our new house would stand on and that my mother should be the one to point her finger and say, "Build it there."

Her face lit up like a happy schoolgirl's, but she looked at my father and said, "Oh, Ed! I wonder if I'll ever be able to decide on just one spot."

Grace, the teacher, spoke up, "You go ahead, Peg, and take all day if you want to. Iris and I'll ride herd on the kids, so you won't have to hurry back."

"Can I go?" I asked anxiously. "I could help a lot."

"Sure," my father said, smiling at my mother. "I'll need someone to hold the tapeline and pound in the stakes. Get your boots on. It'll be wet up there now that the snow's melted."

It was a good thing the weather was so warm, for my mother took a long time deciding about her new house. The general location was a spot close by the creek bank and about fifty yards in from the town road that crossed the valley at that point.

"I always like a house to face the early morning sun," she said.

My father agreed. "And then the porch'll get the afternoon shade and some shelter from that everlasting west wind."

She walked slowly about the little knoll, standing in various places and staring off into the distance. My father took me by the shoulder and guided me over to the sprawling log pile where we both found comfortable seats on the rough bark.

"It's a tough job deciding just where to build your house," he confided to me. "So we'll sit still here and keep quiet if it takes her all day."

Finally, she stopped at a spot close by the stream bank and turned to face the west. Sitting behind her, we could see, as she did, the patch of rough uncut grass, the deep irrigation ditch, and the brown stubble of meadow and pasture beyond, stretching all the way to the steeply climbing foothills with their dark forests of pine and fir. Soaring above were the red and grey and ochre rocks that capped the high Rockies shining under their cover of early snow.

But in her mind's eye, she confessed on the way home, she was looking ahead to the soft grass of early summer, the irrigation ditch running full of sparkling water, prim rows of vegetables streaking the black loam of the garden, and the lush green meadows to the foothills and mountains beyond.

She bent down and with a small stick scratched a cross in the damp earth at her feet.

"I'd like to have the house built so the kitchen sink is right here, with a wide window above it."

"And that's where they'll be," my father promised.

I felt important as I held the tapeline and then tried to pound in the stakes with futile blows from a claw hammer. My father let me struggle for a while, then came over and drove them deep and solid with a couple of blows from the back of his ax.

Later we walked down the road to the bridge across the stream and back up the opposite side, where we spent a long time trying to decide about the barns and corrals. But most of the time my mother's thoughts and eyes were marooned on the other stream bank, where her house was going to be.

There were no cellars or foundations under our western log houses; thus, the business of building started at once. The first tier of logs to outline the house was laid directly on the hard-packed ground. Notches were cut in them to take the floor joists, then the building began to rise, log on log. But after the first three tiers were laid, the building process was halted. The logs, too heavy for two men to lift any higher into place, were cut and dressed, ready for their allotted places in the wall, then marked and piled on one side to wait for the house-raising, which would take place one day early the following spring.

All winter the men worked whenever the weather permitted, carefully measuring each log before notching the ends to fit with its neighbor. The weather side of the log was trimmed and roughly straightened with an ax. But the indoor side was carefully dressed with broadax and adz to make a fairly smooth wall for the room it would enclose. The tangy yellow wood of the freshly hewn logs, set off by the white mortar chinking, would make a fine inner wall, though my father hoped to lath and plaster it some day.

It was a wonderful winter for me since I was allowed to accompany the men every Saturday, weather permitting. My father, by now an expert at finding chores for me to do, kept me busy and out from underfoot. I rode the logs to hold them steady while the two-man, crosscut saw snored back and forth, throwing out squirts of pale sawdust and filling the air with the heady smell of fresh-cut pine. There were also errands to be run and snow to be shoveled, but mostly I picked up the thick broadaxed chips and the scrap blocks sawed from the logs, carried them across the twin-log bridge, and piled them in a corner of the cabin—food for its greedy sheet-iron stove. Lunch time was best of all. We sat around the fire on nail kegs or blocks of wood, talking and eating the badly scorched sandwiches that resulted from poor judgment in toasting them on the red-hot stove. The chipped agate coffeepot boiled away noisily, sending up clouds of steam and powerful coffee smells. I was allowed a small cup of the thick black brew—strong enough, my cousin Frank claimed, to paralyze a yearling colt.

The colder days kept me in the cabin, nursing the fire and collecting smashed fingernails and an assortment of cuts and bruises as I built strange looking toys and bits of furniture at the workbench under the window. My favorite occupation, though, was running the new tool grinder. It was totally different from the old grindstone that I so hated to turn. I sat on a metal seat and pedaled a sprocket wheel and chain just like a bicycle, but instead of speeding along a road, I turned a small emery wheel at high speed. When tools were sharpened on it, long strings of red and white sparks shot out, each spark ending in a tiny explosion. I pedaled this thing for hours at a time, occasionally earning my father's wrath when I wore creases in the face of the stone or chipped its square corners. Quitting time always came too soon for me. Then the horses were hitched to the bobsled, in which we slid quietly across the prairie snow, arriving home in time to finish the evening chores before dark.

By mid-March we were ready for the day of the house-raising. The neighbors came from miles around. Everyone worked with a will, and despite the joking and horseplay, the walls rose steadily. At first the men just lined up along a log, picked it up, and set it in its proper place. As the wall grew higher, poles were laid at a slant from the ground to the highest log. The logs were then hauled up this incline, first rolled by hand and later pulled up by ropes and dropped into place. An experienced axman straddled each corner, and if the notched ends did not mesh properly, a few clips with a razor-sharp ax quickly fixed them. This was the day when all the careful planning and precise cutting and fitting paid off. There were almost no delays caused by wrong measurements or sloppy workmanship, and as the walls rose, so did my father's prestige as an axman and builder. Charlie Rappold summed up the general opinion when he commented to his hoisting gang as the twelfth and last log was locked snugly into place on the top of the wall, "I've helped roll up a lot of logs hereabouts, but for a house as big as this one, this went together slicker than any I can remember."

By midafternoon the last log was up and the rough frames for the windows and doors were spiked into place. The house was now ready for its roof and the logrollers were ready for the huge dinner waiting for them at the lower ranch.

Normally, the logs forming the gable ends of a building, axed off to conform with the pitch of the roof, continued on up to the peak. After the rafters and ridge poles were in place, the roof boards were nailed to them ready to be covered with shingles, asphalt roofing, and often in earlier times, dirt.

But the roof over our new house was to be hipped, that is, pitched in at all sides with no gabled ends; so it had to be framed by a good carpenter using sawmill-cut rafters. The man we hired to do this was a tough old Swede who lived with his work-worn wife in a tar papered house on a nearby homestead. He was disappointed when the roof was completed and my father decided to finish the remaining carpenter work on the house himself, and he made some unflattering predictions about the final results. Sometime later, when the house was finished, he was driving by and stopped to talk. My father, proud of his work, invited him to come in and look it over, which he did, slowly and methodically. He noted without comment the smooth, level floors, the plumb walls and partitions, the tight-set windows, and the doors that swung easily and fitted snugly.

"What do you think of it?" my father had prodded him, as he settled himself in his buggy ready to leave.

The old Swede looked thoughtfully at the house, then spat a stream of brown tobacco juice over the wagon wheel.

"Well," he drawled, "anyone who hangs curtains over a set of fine, square windows like those has sure ruin't a good house." And he drove off without another word.

Except for some time lost when the grain crop had to be planted, the work of finishing the interior of the house progressed rapidly. By the time the spring rains arrived, the floors were down and the partitions and ceilings were in place. "Old Man Moon," one of our hired men, had somewhere in his random wanderings learned something about bricklaying. He did a fine job of laying up our two brick chimneys even though he was blind in one eye and always wore a derby hat and black cutaway coat at his work. The day he finished the second chimney he came down off the roof, walked into the kitchen, climbed up a stepladder to the stovepipe hole in the chimney, and let out a long mournful howl. My father, sitting by the sink on a nail keg and glowering at his balky kitchen plumbing, gave him a startled look. Without saying a word, Moon then dragged the ladder to the living room chimney, where he climbed up and repeated the performance. I edged over by my father, feeling sure the old coot had gone stark-staring crazy. My father looked kind of uneasy, too, and got up off the nail keg when old Moon came back into the kitchen.

"I can always tell by the echo," he said, "when I howl up a chimney if it'll draw right. These two are going to work fine."

The knotty problem about water was not yet solved, however. Something had to be done. My father kept talking about digging a well, while all my mother could think about was the shiny brass faucet in her father's house in Helena.

"Once you dig that well," she told him, "I'll be stuck with running outdoors for every pail of water I use for the rest of my life. You can figure out something better than that, Ed. I know you can."

"Sure," he answered sarcastically, "I'll order a faucet from

Sears tomorrow. And when it comes, I'll screw it on the wall over the sink, hook it to the well with some pipe, and that real smart water will crawl up that pipe and run into your sink."

My mother just snorted and went on patching the knees of my other pair of overalls, while he, in desperation, began once more thumbing through the hardware section of the new mail-order catalog. Something caught his eye, and he reread the item several times. Then he sat quietly for a long time, staring at the house plan. Later, while my mother was busy getting the little kids washed up and off to bed, he got out the pen and ink, carefully filled out an order blank, wrote out a check, and sealed them both up in a Sears-Roebuck envelope. He went outside with it, and I figured he was going to the bunkhouse and tell Frank to ride to town with it the next morning in order to catch the early morning mail stage. He came back in humming —off key as usual.

Toward the end of June, except for the water, the house was ready for its proud owners. The porch, running full length across the front of the house and supported by nine factory-turned posts, stood ready for the coat of paint that it never did get. Even the garden had been plowed and planted, its rows faintly marked by the sprouting seeds. When the subject of water was brought up, my father would just look smug and say he was thinking about it.

For some time now the latch on the granary door had been broken, and everyone was too busy to fix it; a heavy piece of drive-shaft from the threshing rig was propped against it to keep it closed. One evening, while helping my mother get chicken feed from the grain bin, I somehow dropped the heavy iron bar across her foot. Her screams and my yells brought my father on the run. After carrying her to the house and looking at the rapidly swelling foot, he sent Frank racing off to town for the doctor. Shortly after dark he returned with the news that the doctor was over at Bynum on a baby case and that he would come as soon as possible, which turned out to be the afternoon of the next day. After examining the purple, puffed-up instep, he concluded that maybe the bones were broken—or maybe they weren't. She should soak it in epsom salts, keep strictly off it for a couple of weeks and see what happened.

She was heartbroken. "I've got so much to do up at the new house," she wailed. "How will it ever be ready to move into by the first of July if I can't walk?"

My father suggested getting Nettie Pfeiffer to come and help finish up. Nettie was a young married friend and neighbor who often came to help out when things got out of hand.

"Well, all right," my mother agreed. "But I'll have to change everything around afterwards. You know Nettie and I don't always see things the same way."

A couple of days later the mysterious crate arrived from Sears-Roebuck and was quietly sneaked up to the new house. Each day Nettie and the men left early in the morning and returned late in the afternoon, Frank and my father sweat-stained and filthy dirty.

"What are you two doing up there?" my mother wanted to know. "Mining?"

"Kind of," my father answered. "Actually we're digging a ditch over to that London water main so we can hook up your kitchen faucet." And he ducked as she wadded up the shirt she was mending and hurled it at his head.

I was dying of curiosity and kept coaxing my father to let me go along with them. Finally he gave in, but he warned me what to expect if I opened my big mouth afterward.

On reaching the new house next morning, I discovered they had dug a ten-foot deep open well part way under the house and beneath the kitchen sink. The sink was in place, and a sturdy shelf had been bolted to its right side and a hole cut through the floor directly underneath it to receive the water pipe. On the floor were the contents of the wooden crate; a small bright red pitcher pump, a length of water pipe, and a wellpoint. It was this wellpoint that had solved our problem. It consisted of a short piece of perforated water pipe covered with a fine mesh copper screening. A sharp steel point was welded to one end and the other screwed onto the water pipe leading up to the pump.

First, they fastened the pump to its shelf. Then the two men assembled the pipe and point, and dropped it through the hole in the floor and into the pool of water that had collected in the well. The pipe was now screwed to the pump, and we were ready to try it out. Frank grabbed the handle and worked it vigorously. Nothing happened.

"Hell," my father said. "I forgot you have to prime it."

He poured some water into the cylinder; Frank pumped, and sure enough, water poured from its spout.

"We'll take turns pumping as fast as we can and see if the water holds up," my father decided.

After ten minutes of steady pumping, the water level remained unchanged.

"I'll be damned," my father said softly. "Looks like it's going to work!"

The men went out and started filling in the wellhole as the catalog claimed you could. As the level of thick mud rose in the well, Frank wondered out loud if the point would really work in it. My father's confidence was at a high level, and he was pretty sure it would. However, he finally decided that they had better have some real proof before they went any further with the filling in.

They went inside, and Frank started pumping. He was rewarded with some labored gasping, a thin trickle of muddy water, then nothing. The thing had quit dead.

My father stared wrathfully at the little red pump. "Damn it all!" he said. "I thought we had it." Then he really started to swear but stopped abruptly when Nettie spoke through the living room doorway. "Don't see where all that swearing's going to help any."

His face reddened. "Sorry, Nettie, I forgot you were here." Then to Frank, "We'll have to take that . . . blasted . . . thing apart, clean the point in the creek, and try again."

Half an hour later they tried again. Still plugged. After about the fifth try it was *still* plugged. They gave up. My father sat down on a nail keg, swearing softly under his breath. Finally his common sense took over, and he scowled thoughtfully at the invisible well under the floor.

"I think I've got it," he said, jumping up. "That point can only work in gravel, I'll bet. This heavy loam just clogs it up.

"We'll dig out the mud, dump in a couple loads of gravel, and see."

By late afternoon all was ready. This time the water came freely but dirty. It gradually cleared up, however, and finally ran crystal clear. At last we had it—indoor plumbing!

Everything was in readiness now: the kitchen linoleum was laid; a huge black iron cooking range squatted in its place all hooked up to Old Man Moon's wonderful chimney; the floors were painted a light brown, and the woodwork in the kitchen and pantry a practical French grey. Nettie had washed and polished the windows and hung the new curtains my mother had spent so many happy hours making last winter. She had also unpacked the gleaming parlor furniture, dusted and polished it, and arranged it carefully in its new room—all ready for my mother to rearrange without delay.

My father had built and painted a huge kitchen table, with long drop leaves on each side. And also—for my particular benefit, I thought—a woodbox "about the size of a boxcar," as Frank had observed to me as he watched his Uncle Ed hammer it together. I had filled it—without protest for once—with freshly split, sweet-smelling pine.

Moving day was the mad scramble that moving days always are. Nettie and we kids rode up on the first load. My mother was the last to leave the old house, checking every shelf and cupboard to be sure nothing was left behind, and finally supervising the final sweeping, closing of windows, and latching of doors.

"Your sister Minnie isn't going to arrive here and find this house a mess," she said stubbornly to my father.

Convinced at last that everything was done, she climbed up into the buggy, carefully protecting her bad leg, and sat down beside my father. Then they followed the last wagonload as it jolted along the ruts leading to the new ranch.

My father stopped the buggy close by the new porch, jumped out and held out his arms.

"Come on, Peg," he said, "I'm going to carry you into your new home."

We were all standing on the porch—my two sisters and

baby brother, and myself, along with Frank and Leo, Nettie, and of course, Old Man Moon—grinning happily at each other, waiting to see her face when she first entered her new kitchen.

She looked around, blushing like a bride, and protested primly that she could "still walk!"

But he persisted, "Come on, Peg. Be a sport! Gosh, I don't know when I'll get around to build you another house."

Laughing, she stepped carefully over the buggy wheel and dropped into his arms, to be set lightly through the door into her kitchen.

The late afternoon sunlight streamed through the broad double window high in the opposite wall. Her eyes turned slowly, taking in the long table covered with a red and white checkered cloth and decorated with a bowl of pasture roses. The cooking range, freshly blackened and with gleaming nickel-work, stood opposite next to the huge, generously filled wood-box. Beside her, my father's easy chair lounged invitingly in front of the low eastern window. With intent face she slowly hobbled across the room to the kitchen sink, ignoring the bright red pump sitting jauntily by its side, and leaned forward against its iron rim to look through the polished window pane. It was just as she had pictured it: the green grass, the young garden, and beyond, the waving meadowgrass and the soaring mountains. She stood there for a long moment—just looking.

At last her eyes turned to the pump and her face lit up. "So that's it!" she said softly. Her fingers stroked the cold metal handle as if seeking assurance that it was real. Then taking the tin dipper from its nail above the sink and pumping with brisk strokes, she filled it to overflowing with sparkling cold well water. First she took a sip, then a swallow, and finally, tipping her head far back, she drained it.

Only then did she turn around and look at us.

"It's wonderful, Ed," she said. "I don't know where you're getting that water from, but it sure isn't coming from any damn London water main."

We followed as she hobbled through the rest of the rooms, examining, exclaiming, finally winding up in the middle of the parlor floor. We all crowded through the door as she slowly turned on her heel and surveyed the little room—the arrangement of the polished furniture, the ax-finished log walls and gleaming windows framed with starched white curtains, and the carefully swept turkey-red carpet.

Finally she looked at us with a puzzled frown. "You know," she said, "everything—the whole house—looks so darn nice I don't think I'll have to change a thing."

School Days

USUALLY EVERYONE ON THE RANCH was in a hurry to get to the supper table and start eating. Grownups and kids alike were starving by suppertime, and my mother was hurrying to serve up the food hot. But this early September evening was different. Our new teacher had arrived from the East an hour ago and had gone to her room to rest. Now we were all excitedly waiting for her to appear for supper.

My father and the two hired men were shaved and combed, and even though it wasn't Saturday night wore clean shirts. I hadn't been able to get away with my usual "lick and promise" but was thoroughly scrubbed and laundered, as were my two sisters. And my mother had taken time to curl her hair, powder her face, and put on a fresh dress. We stood around the kitchen table waiting to begin supper, our eyes glued to the closed living room door. At last it was pushed slowly open, and she stood there—smiling, blue eyes, golden hair, fashionable clothes—the new teacher. I was six and instantly and hopelessly in love. And tomorrow was my first day of school.

Most of our teachers came from some mysterious place

44

called "back East." They stayed at our ranch and lived with us as members of the family, helping my mother during their spare time and sharing all our activities, even our affection. At least this particular girl did. Perhaps it was she who sparked me with the love of books and interest in learning which I have had ever since I walked across the prairie with her that first morning to school.

Having the teacher live with us had other advantages, too, as well as the disadvantage of having to be on our good behavior more of the time than most kids. For example, I was never scolded for being late for school. If I was late, so was the teacher. Books were scarce on ranches, and if anyone was apt to have one that we might borrow, it was the teacher. My father, too, reaped one of these benefits, since the best ranch hands for miles around practically stood in line waiting for an opportunity to work and live so close to the schoolma'am.

The school was about a mile from our ranch, straight across the prairie. There was no road, not even a path. My mother, after making sure we were dressed appropriately for the weather, would hand us our five-pound lard pails filled with lunch and head us due north. If we didn't stray, the small building would soon rise up on the horizon to guide us the rest of the way.

The school was a twelve-by-twenty-foot log cabin with a lean-to in back for storing firewood. It stood alone with its two one-holers in a one-acre yard surrounded by a barbed wire fence. To the west towered the Rocky Mountains of Glacier National Park. Eastward forty miles away were the blue outlines of the Sweetgrass Hills. To the north and south the rolling prairie stretched to the horizon.

In my preschool days I was familiar with the building only as a sort of public gathering place. I had been there with my parents to dances and box socials and Christmas entertainments. I even attended my first church service there, which was conducted by a wandering priest from one of the Catholic missions in the area.

Building a school in those early days was a community effort. One rancher would donate the land; another or several of the others would haul logs from the pine forests farther up the mountain and dump them on the site. Then various ranch hands who were handy with tools would erect the building and fence the yard to keep the range cattle out. Even the collecting of school taxes had to be done by the interested parties, because many of the surrounding ranchers took the attitude, "Let them as has kids, educate them."

Inside, the walls were of undressed logs notched at the corners and chinked with mortar. The roof was made of wide boards laid across the roof timbers. These boards were sometimes boxed off at the eaves to hold in place the sixteen inches of dirt often used as roofing material. This made an excellent roof in dry weather. But during spells of persistent rain, the water seeped through, and our study and recitation periods were interrupted by frequent dashes from one spot to another to escape a muddy shower bath.

Also someone had miscalculated the flooring, and as a result most of the boards didn't quite reach the wall, leaving an irregular gap of several inches around the outer edges of the room. In winter the snow drifted up under the log walls and through this space, and a snowbank lined the walls, sometimes for days, until the wood fire in the sheet-iron stove gained the upper hand and melted it away. This stove was located in the center of the room with the desks placed as closely around it as the heat would allow, and since we kept on all our winter clothing except caps and mittens during severe cold spells, the scent of scorched leather and overheated wool pervaded the school during most of the winter months. In spring and fall a trip to the privy was something of a field excursion and was enjoyed to the limit of the teacher's patience. But in winter nothing but dire necessity drove us to those snowbound outhouses.

Each new teacher was allowed to use whatever methods she liked best, and we became quite flexible in adjusting to different ways of doing the same thing. I remember one teacher from Montreal who was highly criticized for using Canadian textbooks, but for the most part there was little interference from the outside. In fact, my father, who was a trustee and was self-educated and well read beyond most of our neighbors, was the only one I remember visiting us during a school session. One of our teachers who loved to read became a favorite with her students because she would stretch the noon and recess periods out longer and longer to allow herself time to read her book until gradually the actual school sessions had practically disappeared. My father, riding by one day and seeing us all out in the schoolyard playing at two o'clock in the afternoon, became suspicious and decided to call on the teacher. School became a little more formal after that.

One thing my mother worried about while we were walking to and from school was wild cattle. A man on horseback had nothing to fear on the open prairie, but a person on foot was looked upon with suspicion and hostility by range cattle and was sometimes badly mauled by them; so we had orders to stay close to the line fence that crossed the prairie at that point. Only the worst kind of weather would get us a ride in a bobsled or spring wagon. My father would open the kitchen door and look out on a wild, rainy or snowy morning and say, "I've got a lot of things to do today. I guess you kids can make it all right." And we always did.

Maybe my father sounded a little offhand about the weather, but he really wasn't because he knew how tricky our high prairie climate could be and how fast it could change. One January we had several heavy falls of snow, accompanied by steady freezing winds that drifted the coulees and swales level-full, and it was only by zigzagging along the windswept ridges that we were able to walk to school.

My father made his usual weather inspection one sunny morning and then came back to the kitchen where my mother was energetically buttoning up the last button and making sure we all had our mittens. "Looks like a nice day," he said to the teacher. "Fifteen above and no wind. But I smell a change in the air, so if a storm blows up don't try to walk home. Someone will come for you."

"You must be mistaken," Ruth said as she looked out of the window. "It's beautiful out."

"The first thing you learn about Montana weather," my mother interrupted flatly, "is never to trust it!"

By the time we reached the low school building, half buried among the snowdrifts, a strong wind was blowing from the west. The teacher looked at the thermometer by the door as we went in and whistled with surprise.

"Why it's above freezing!" she said and added in amazement, "it smells and feels like spring."

"I'll bet we're going to have a chinook," I said importantly.

"A chinook? You mean when the wind blows all the snow away?"

"Naw!" I said, a little disgusted with her. "It doesn't *blow* it away. It's hot. It *melts* the snow."

All morning the warm wind roared down the mountain slopes, and the sun shone hot from a cloudless sky. Ruth kept making trips to inspect the thermometer, and when it read sixty she was popeyed with disbelief. I watched one of the fenceposts most of the morning, and it seemed to be growing steadily up out of the blanket of snow. By noon the two top strands of wire were in the clear, and the windswept places on the prairie were brown again.

I arrived home that evening carrying my coat and soaking wet up to my waist. The prairie was traced with small brooks that I had waded in, and I had tested the depth of water in some ponds that were forming in the low spots. Our placid, ice-bound creek was now a raging torrent that threatened to carry away the twin-log footbridge that spanned it. By the time I had been thoroughly scolded by my mother, gotten into some dry clothes, and filled that always empty woodbox, the sun had set, and there was a distinct chill in the air again.

When my father came in from his evening chores, he set the pail of milk on the pantry shelf and grinned at Ruth, who was setting the supper table. "Told you we were going to have a change in the weather today."

The teacher laughed, "About four o'clock I was expecting to see you coming across the fields in a rowboat instead of a bobsled."

Sometime during the night the thermometer hit zero again. The sun was shining bright and cold when we left for school next morning, slipping and sliding across a world that was sheathed in ice. The pond that had formed in the low place across the road yesterday was now a smooth glaze. I would hurry home tonight, I planned, and try out my new Ace clamp-on skates that Aunt Annie had given me for Christmas.

By 1909 my parents and a few of our neighbors had come to the conclusion that the old log schoolhouse was not worth keeping up any longer. Besides it was too isolated for the younger children to walk to. It was decided to build a new school in a better location. They worked hard to raise enough money and to convince some of the people that a new school was needed. Ties of friendship were badly strained in many instances. The most effective arguments in favor of a new school were not its educational facilities but its use for community affairs. To remind the bachelor ranchers of the advantages for meeting the new schoolma'ams and the few unattached females in the area was the best way to bring forth a "yes" vote from them.

At last the necessary few hundred dollars were collected, and my Uncle George, who lived in the most central location, donated a plot of land a few hundred yards from his ranch house. Because it was to be a no-expense-spared job, a real carpenter and his helper from the town of Valier, twenty-five miles away, were hired to build it. They would live at the ranch until it was finished. The building was started in the fall, and by the time it was completed, we were well into one of our early and sometimes violent Montana winters.

But there it was! Our schoolhouse—a building larger than the old log one, built with real lumber and sheathed in respectable white clapboards. There was even a small cupola on top but no bell. The cupola was just for effect. Inside, the matched wainscoting reached to the ceiling and was covered with two coats of dazzling gloss-white paint. The new blackboard covered the entire wall back of the teacher's desk, and a new extra large sheet-iron stove dominated the opposite end of the room. The crowning glory of it all was a big seven-day pendulum clock with "Regulator" painted in gold on its glass door.

A great combination dance and box-social was planned to dedicate the new school. The women worked for weeks, decorating with ribbons and colored paper the lunch baskets that were

to be auctioned off to start raising money for the pump organ
my mother and the teacher had picked out of the Montgomery
Ward catalog. Ranch hands bought new levis, brightly colored
flannel shirts, and—their one concession to fashion—brilliant
silk neckerchiefs. The neckerchief served a dual purpose. Besides being a reflection of the male ego, it was used to overcome
the shortage of ladies at the dances. Out our way the men out-
numbered the women ten to one, and by tying a bandanna on
their left arms, the men who had agreed to be ladies in the
dancing could be identified.

The big day finally arrived and with it the worst storm of
the year! The wind blew with hurricane force, driving the snow
in blinding clouds across the face of the land. There was a
steady low-pitched roar of the wind, accompanied by the hissing
sound of ice crystals hitting against, and sliding across, the frozen snow on the ground. The ranch families spent the day
watching the weather, their hopes rising with every lull in the
wind, only to have them dashed down with each new and more
furious blast of wind. By dusk all sensible people had abandoned their plans for the party.

The new school had been built down the valley from our
place and within sight of Uncle George and Aunt Minnie's
house. That morning I had been sent down to their house on
some errand, but as the fury of the storm had increased, Aunt
Minnie was afraid I couldn't make it home and decided I
should stay with them all night. I had watched the storm from
the window all afternoon, turning reluctantly away when she
mentioned that it was my bedtime, for I was still hoping someone might be foolish enough to come.

Just then the sound of barking dogs and shouting voices
came from down by the bunkhouse. By the light of its lanterns I
could make out a bobsled filled with hay and blankets and a
dozen or so young folks from the ranches upstream who had
somehow made it through the storm and sounded ready for a
fight if the party did not go on as planned. So in spite of the
disappointments—the weather, the missing fiddle player, and
the late hour—four ranch girls, one middle-aged aunt and uncle,
one proud carpenter and his helper, a dozen carefree cowboys,

and one eight-year-old boy decided to have a shindig after all.

Snow swished around the corners of the eaves, and the wind blew down the chimney of the new schoolhouse that night until smoke and flames flared out of every crack and cranny of the sheet-iron stove. The oil lamps flickered in their brackets, but the dance went on to the music of two mouth organs and the beat of a high-heeled cowboy boot on the floor. At midnight coffee and sandwiches were served, and our new schoolhouse was duly dedicated.

Chores

WHEN I THINK OF THE WORD "CHORES," I automatically think of a woodbox and my mother's voice saying, "Mick, the woodbox is empty." While my father often threatened but seldom punished, my mother relied on instant and drastic action; so by the time I was eight years old, I kept a pretty sharp eye on that woodbox and made sure it was reasonably well filled at all times.

It seemed to me that my mother was very reckless about her use of firewood. She was quite small but loaded with energy, and her approach to a stoking job on the kitchen range always gave me a sinking feeling. Moving briskly to the stove, she would lift off a lid, peer in, and remove the other two lids with

a great clattering. After some vigorous poking around with the
lid lifter, she piled the firebox full of my beautiful, freshly split
wood. Then she would bang the lids back on and slam all the
drafts wide open; and I would stand helplessly by, listening to
all my hard work go roaring up the chimney to disappear with a
cloud of smoke and sparks into the clean northwest Montana
air.

The wood to supply this generous habit of my mother's
came from the pine and fir forests of the main range of the
Rockies about eight miles to the west. It was mostly blown-
down trees that seasoned out on the ground in the dry air.
Sometime in late summer several wagonloads of these logs were
hauled down and piled in back of the house to be sawed up
later into stove wood. Usually the men camped up there a night
or two while they skidded out the logs, and every year I tried to
talk my parents into letting me go along. But my mother was
sure I'd get killed by a mountain lion or a grizzly bear, or more
likely still, smashed by a falling tree.

And not without some reason on her part, for there were
occasional raids on range stock by mountain lions, resulting in
the loss of calves and colts. Once a young neighbor, Cliff Gordon, hunting up there on horseback—a cowboy never walked if
he could ride—came around a huge rock and ran almost head-
on into a grizzly going in the opposite direction. The smart cow-
pony never hesitated a second but bucked Cliff off and went
tearing down the mountain at about eighty miles an hour. Cliff
was on his feet and running at the second bounce and beat the
bear to a tree by about two jumps. He spent most of the day
perched up in the branches watching the angry beast tear up his
bedroll, smash his rifle, and as a final insult chew his brand new
Stetson hat into small pieces and spit them out on the ground.
Finally, the bear wandered off, and Cliff made a fast trip home
on foot, looking back over his shoulder most of the way.

When I was about nine, I made my first trip up to the
mountains for logs. We got an early start and had camp set up
by noon. By evening the men had skidded up a large pile of logs
ready for loading the next day. In those times most men were
passable cooks, and soon we were sitting on logs eating a tasty

meal of steaks, fried potatoes, and sourdough biscuits. During the meal everyone got to lying about how much wood he could cut and how fast he could fell a tree. A hot argument got started between Nolan, our hired man, and Leo, my cousin; after supper, with still some daylight left, they decided to settle the dispute. Two trees of equal size were selected and the two arguers set to work. We were closely watching the sweating axmen as they neared the finish, when there was a sudden crack of Leo's tree, and then my father's frantic voice yelling, "Run, Mick! Run!" Automatically I did the same as Cliff's horse—took off down the mountain at full speed. Of course, the tree was falling the same way, as they usually do, and it was a close race. I vaguely remember my father pulling me out of a tangle of fallen branches and thorn bushes, scratched and bloody, but probably the least scared of all.

The hired men always had to saw and split the stove wood, a job they thoroughly detested. One of the chores I never minded was riding the logs to help keep them from rolling, since I could listen in on the conversation of the two men pulling the crosscut saw. This added considerably to my education, some of which was a closely kept secret from my mother.

After the wood was sawed and split, it was my job to take it into the house. It looked like a mountain to me, and it didn't seem as if it could ever be used up. But, in fact, it vanished as fast as our ten-foot snowbanks in a chinook wind. That big fire-eating kitchen range had an appetite like a locomotive.

However, the woodbox did give a bonus for all the hard work it demanded of me. An expression my father used to describe someone who was not really sick but just pleasantly so, was "He's sick abed in the woodbox." I wasn't often sick abed, but I did spend a lot of time in the woodbox. I liked to sit in it on a cold winter afternoon or evening, soaking up the glowing heat of the stove, listening to the crackling and roaring of the fire, watching the orange flames flickering through the chinks and cracks of the firebox, and dreaming the carefree dreams of a small boy.

I was never able to understand my mother's obsession to get her washing done. Come "hell or high water," the clothes had to be washed every Saturday when we kids were home to help. My older sister, Iris, was pretty good at laundry work, but I was just a power supplier and a stocking turner. Because of our pump, I didn't have to carry water from the well or creek. But I did have to operate the handle of the pump, and many a blister I collected while filling the washboiler, the warming tank on the back of the stove, the bread pan for heating rinse water, and the two big tubs (one for rinsing and one for blueing). My mother always worked at top speed, and we had to step on it to keep up with her. There was usually some confusion and an occasional disaster, like the time the kitchen was flooded with hot soapy water when a carelessly tightened plug fell out of the washing tub, or the day my sister's fingers got slightly squashed in the wringer roll. (How did I know she wouldn't let go in time when I gave the handle that little extra yank?)

While I was turning the wringer crank, I at least had someone to talk to, but when working the washing machine, I was alone. I was supposed to turn that handle for at least fifteen minutes. I rotated the tub back and forth, endlessly back and forth, while the clock stood still. But at last it was done, and I would look hopefully at my mother only to get a hard look and, "You know you still have to turn the stockings." By this time the tub would be half full of chilly, slightly thickened and heavily scummed hard water, rank and dark grey in color. Down in there were about a thousand long black knitted cotton stockings, all intertwined and interlocked into one great, revolting mass. I would carefully dip my hand in, grasp one of the awful things, and pull. It would come out with much reluctance and stretching, somewhat the way an angleworm does when you pull it from its burrow. Then sliding my arm down its clammy length, I would grab the toe and with one quick jerk turn it inside out. It was ready to be rinsed. And I had only nine hundred and ninty-nine more left to do.

After the struggle of getting the clothes clean, there was the business of getting them dry. Hung out in winter, they immediately froze as stiff as corpses and usually wound up, late in the day, draped over chairs and benches around the stove. In the rainy season they hung on the line for days, my mother hoping the sun would struggle forth long enough to get them at least partly dry.

During one of these June rainy spells, the day had started clear, but as she hung out the freshly wrung clothes, it began to rain hard again, and they immediately soaked up tons of water. Just as she turned to come back into the house, the clothesline broke, dropping everything into the dirt. I had observed the mishap through the kitchen window and debated so long with myself about going out and lending a hand that she was just picking up the last muddy sheet when I came up and asked, "Need any help, Ma?" All that saved my life was the fact that she was wearing my father's gum boots and an old ten-gallon hat, both several sizes too large. Turning and starting for me with a cry of fury, she got her feet tangled and fell sprawling. By the time she had dragged herself upright and slapped the hat back out of her eyes, I was across the bridge and nearing the horse barn, where I had a hiding place in the hayloft that no one had yet found.

I also used this hiding place to get out of doing dishes, though I resorted to it only in extreme cases, such as when company came or after one of my mother's baking orgies. There was something about dishwashing and clothes-washing that brought out the worst in me. I always looked on them as woman's work and fiercely resented having anything to do with them. Iris and I wrangled almost continually while doing dishes, so in the interest of peace and quiet, I was excused at a fairly early age, the schoolteacher and my younger sister Lucy getting the job.

Our vegetable garden was an important part of our food supply; none of the chores connected with it were taken lightly by my parents. It was located in back of the house and extended a hundred yards or so along the bank of the creek. The annual floods had built a deep layer of silted loam that was very productive, especially of weeds. During the rainy weather I often found myself pulling pigweed as tall as I was. Though we could sometimes buy potatoes from some of the neighbors, we had either to raise our own carrots, beets, and cabbages as well as all the other summer green vegetables or go without. When the weather turned dry, I carried whole lakes of water trying to save the wilting beans and lettuce and peas and even the spinach, which I loathed. Several times during the summer the potato plants had to be doused with Paris green. This was usually my job and one I couldn't cheat on, for if I missed a plant, the bugs promptly ate it up. In the fall, after school and on Saturdays, we kids picked up the potatoes the men had dug, a job that too often wound up in a pitched battle with potatoes as ammunition. Pat, my next younger brother, was a deadly marksman with them; as a result we often carried an assortment of black eyes and bruises. But before winter weather arrived, we always managed to fill the root cellar—minus, of course, a few of my father's prized potatoes.

The milk cows on our ranch were converted range stock, and milking them was a job that required strength and animal know-how beyond my years. Therefore, I never got into it much except as an interested spectator. Although practically all early Montana ranchers refused to have anything to do with milk cows, as the small mountains of evaporated milk cans rusting away behind the log houses testified, my father always kept a few. Since any cowboy or ranch hand worth his salt would rather be dragged by his horse than caught milking a cow, the milking fell pretty much to my father.

The cows were wild, mean, and suspicious, and "breaking them in" could provide fun and excitement—especially for the watcher. One day my father and Leo found one of them on the Birch Creek range standing over her dead new-born calf. Since she looked well equipped for supplying milk for the family, they decided to drive her home. By the time they reached the ranch, men and horses were ready to drop from exhaustion, but the cow was still full of fight. After supper we all went down to the corral to see her. She was a big brindled cow, rawboned and rangy, and sporting a rack of long, sharp horns. She also had a distinct cast in one eye.

"Why, she looks just like Mrs. Perkins!"

Mrs. Perkins, my mother explained, was a cross-eyed woman with an uncertain temper and a mean disposition whom she had worked for as a girl. The name was a perfect fit.

"Now," my father announced, "it's time Mrs. Perkins

found out about milking."

We all perched in a long row on the top bar of the corral to watch.

He started out confidently enough. "I'll have her eating out of my hand in no time," he told us. "All you have to do is get them to trust you."

"*So-o-o,* Boss," he said, moving toward her. Mrs. Perkins backed away. He tried again. Each time he came within ten feet of her, she would cock her eye at him and either back swiftly away or start pawing the ground, ready to charge.

"Leo," he said, finally giving up, "go get your lariat. We'll have to rope her."

Leo returned and, taking my father's place in the corral, tossed the loop over the cow's horns. Mrs. Perkins charged like a shot, and Leo dropped the rope and barely made it over the top bar. Seeing that he was safe, we all whooped with laughter. He really had looked funny sailing over that six-foot fence and trying to watch the cow at the same time.

When we had stopped laughing and Leo had caught his breath he turned to my father. "All right, Uncle Ed," he said. "It's your turn now."

After several tries they got hold of the rope and dragged the protesting animal into a corner of the corral and tied her up short. This gave her less room to maneuver in and took care of her murderous horns, but she was far from licked. Gathering together his equipment, which consisted of a rickety milking stool and a large tin pail, my father cautiously approached his victim with a series of *So-o-o Bosses* and other soothing noises, followed up with gentle handpats. The cow, glaring at him out of her misplaced eye, edged away and jammed herself up tight against the fence. This gave him his chance. He gingerly squatted down and slipped the stool under him, clamped the pail tightly between his knees and reached out to start work. Wild range cows are extremely sensitive about such proceedings, and Mrs. Perkins was no exception. She kicked so hard and so fast, no one actually saw it happen. The pail arched across the corral and clanged to a stop against the fence. My father scrambled to his feet out of a cloud of dust, mad and swearing.

Mrs. Perkins gave him a hard look then started chewing her cud. He glared back at her two crossed eyes and then at the convulsed row of spectators on the fence. Slowly he walked over and picked up his battered hat, knocked off the dust against his leg, and gave us all a sheepish grin, then laughed loudest of all. We hadn't had such a good time since the teacher got chased by a buck sheep and Leo got butted all over the pasture trying to save her. Though Mrs. Perkins eventually became reconciled to her role as a domestic cow and faithfully supplied us with milk for several years, she always remained a free and independent soul, and often added spice to my father's milking chores.

While I was exempt from the actual milking, I did at an early age get the job of going after the cows. This was mostly fun and often took much longer than was necessary. When I went on foot and followed along the creek, there was almost always something strange or new to see. Once when I was lying on my stomach on the creek bank, watching for a fish to stop close enough for me to try to grab it, I noticed a slight movement on a stone out in the riffle. It was a mink fishing for his supper. Crouching in his shiny, dark brown coat, he was now as motionless as the stone he sat on. Suddenly there was a flash of movement, a spray of water, and he was bounding along the stream bank, a wildly flopping trout in his mouth. It all happened with such speed and grace that even though I was watching intently, I almost missed the catch. I often found the nests of grouse and prairie chicken in the thick grass and willow clumps along the creek, and even though I was half-expecting it, the sudden explosion of the bird's wings as it flew up almost almost under my feet always made me jump. Once in a while I'd start up a pair of coyotes who were napping in the shade of a chokecherry bush and have a panicky feeling that maybe they were wolves.

When the cows were farther away I'd go on horseback. There had been a couple of incidents of young boys getting thrown off their horses and fatally dragged because a foot got caught in the stirrup, so all my riding had to be done bareback. If the horse was old and had a high backbone, it could be very painful. I soon learned to sit slightly sideways, and by continually shifting back and forth, I could arrive home fit to sit in a chair at supper. It was great fun to ride at a gallop behind the bawling cows, jumping over buckbrush, dodging badger holes, and encouraging our dog, Monday, to catch any lagging cow by the tail and take a long slide behind her. But I always slowed down well short of the barn so that my father wouldn't see me doing it.

For many years we handled our milk as everyone else did. We used what we needed for the table, and the remainder was poured into wide shallow pans and put on the pantry shelf for the cream to rise. Each morning my mother skimmed the cream from the previous day's milking and put it into a large stone crock. The accumulated cream of several days added up to another chore—churning. Though this was not particularly my job, I was pressed into service often enough to thoroughly hate the sitting still and the monotonous turning of the crank or pounding of the dasher.

One day my father returned from town with a mysterious machine. Ignoring our questions about it, he carefully bolted it to the pantry floor. After he had fitted some shining metal spouts into place and capped it all with a large tank on top, he stepped back, "This," he said, "is a cream separator."

Knowing how he loved to joke, we were all suspicious.

"A cream separator?" I asked. "What the heck's that?"

He explained: you filled the tank with milk and started turning the crank, and when it was going fast enough, you let the milk run through. Blue skim milk was supposed to come out one spout and thick yellow cream out the other.

Nolan had been eyeing the heavy, two-handed crank attached to one side of the machine. "That thing looks like it might turn hard," he said. "Who's going to work it?"

My father's eye roved around the circle of spectators and stopped on me. "Why Mick, of course."

That night we ran our first milking through the separator, and it was an instant success.

I once had an Uncle Charlie who was no admirer of work, and he cautioned me to keep away from things that had handles on them. As time went by, I discovered he had a shrewd mind, for almost everything that had anything to do with chores seemed to have a handle on it somewhere.

But the high-pitched hum and the effortless way this beautiful machine performed its work fascinated me and took much of the drudgery out of this routine chore.

Another thing I noticed was that when anything interesting was going on, I had to carry water, lots of water. Men working in large groups seemed to have a compulsion to stand around drinking water. So whenever we had a roof-shingling, a log-raising, a sheep-shearing, or a threshing, early in the program my father would appear with a couple of water pails.

"Fill these," he would say, "and get them up to the sheep shed. It's going to be a hot day and the boys will be thirsty." I'd pump them nearly full of water from the well and start on the quarter mile hike to the sheep shed. By the time I had finished my trip, the pails were half empty, and from my waist down I was soaking wet and mighty uncomfortable.

I particularly hated shearing time in late June, when it was hot. The sheepshearers, stripped to the waist, clipped furiously and naturally worked up a raging thirst. I would pass down by the shearing pens, reluctantly offering my pails of water. Each man would grab the tin dipper, fill it brimming full, and start gulping it down. At least half the dipperful ran out of the corners of his mouth and splashed off his sweaty, hairy chest. In minutes I'd be on my way back to the house for more water, plotting hopeless revenge with each weary step.

There was always considerable difference of opinion between me and the grownups on which chores were mine. Many of the jobs that seemed to me to be theirs were dumped on me. Even the schoolteacher, backed up by my father, saw to it that I did my share of keeping the school woodbox full and fresh drinking water in the pail. I considered this unfair. The teacher got paid for running the school. Why weren't the chores hers also? Needless to say, I never got very far with this theory. I always thought myself badly overworked, and it's amazing how I found time to get into so many scrapes and have as much fun as I did. I always fell for praise, though, and glowed with pride when my father artfully gave me some special chore. He would say to me as he was leaving in the fall with the threshing rig,

"Don't forget to feed Bugeater and take him down to the creek for water. Remember I'm depending on you." And with a bit of jogging of my memory, I seldom forgot.

Without really understanding it, I knew I was an important and necessary part of our ranch and of the school as well. The teacher not only thoroughly grounded me in the three Rs, but with the enthusiastic help of my family and the whole neighborhood, she made sure I had an advanced education also in a fourth letter—C for chores.

Thrashin' Time

AGAINST MY FATHER'S ORDERS, my sister Iris and I had been swinging each other on the big polegate that opened into the ranch yard. We were sitting now on the top bar of the gate, resting.

"Look! Look!" Iris was pointing. Sure enough there was a little single-seated, high-wheeled car gingerly working its way along the deep-rutted road leading down from the bench across the valley.

"It's Gene Leach's automobile."

"Naw. Can't you see it's red? Leach's is blue. I bet it's the J.I.C. man."

In northwest Montana automobiles and our 1908 brand of roads had as little as possible to do with each other. So when a car approached, it was a source of great excitement for young and old alike.

"If it *is* the J.I.C. man," Iris said, "he'll stay all night, and we can sit up late and listen to them talk."

But my mind was on the car. "He'll give us a ride," I said,

"like the last time. Come on. Let's go tell Ma."

We tumbled off the gate and ran to the house, screaming loud enough for all Teton County to hear, "There's an automobile coming! The J.I.C. man's coming!"

The J.I.C. man was the service representative of the J.I. Case Threshing Machine Company. He came every summer to check over our machine. Last year he had abandoned his usual hired livery rig and appeared in a brand new four-cylinder Reo painted a blinding red, and he had given everyone a breath-taking twenty-mile-an-hour ride down the long lane to the bend in the road and back. Even better than that was the fun of tagging him and my father around all day and listening to them talk "machine." Any kind of machinery had a fascination for me but especially the huge threshing machine, which my father drove from ranch to ranch during two months of the early fall, threshing the ranchers' grain crops.

A couple of weeks ago a large wooden crate of repair parts had arrived by freight from the Case factory. Now Mr. Shaeffer had come to replace the worn parts and check and adjust the whole rig. As they worked, my father, patiently trying to keep me out of the way, invented numerous errands for me to run and finally in desperation turned me loose with a long-spouted oil can and a pail of very black grease. "Oil these bearings here," he directed. "Then put some grease on that big gear." And as a vague afterthought, "Don't get any on your clothes, now."

It was a blissful afternoon. When I tramped into the house with the men for supper, my mother gave me one look and wailed, "My God, Ed! How could you do it? It'll take me a week to clean that kid up."

My father soothed her with his easy laugh and said, winking broadly at Mr. Shaeffer, "He's been a real help, Peg. I don't think we could have finished today without him." Mr. Shaeffer agreed heartily. "Never saw so much grease and oil squirted around in one day in my whole life."

I ate supper in a happy daze.

Before dark we each had our ride. The car, with its soft springs and rubber-shod wheels, carried us along like a magic carpet. Then the men pulled the buggy from the wagon shed and the car took its place because, as Mr. Shaeffer said, "If it gets rained on tonight, it'll take me half the day tomorrow to get it started."

After that, we sat around on the porch listening while the grown folks talked about "back East," where Mr. Shaeffer came from. He told about the St. Louis fair, about cities where automobiles were almost as common as horses (which I could hardly believe), about houses lighted by gas, and people riding around in electric trolley cars. He gave us news of the coming elections, the latest reports on grain and beef prices, and told how Teddy Roosevelt was digging a huge ditch a mile wide and forty miles long across Panama, wherever that was. How I wished that day would never end! I wouldn't have traded it for the Fourth of July, Christmas, and the last day of school—all rolled into one.

Lying just in front of our log house was a forty-acre pasture where we kept the working horses, a few ailing cattle, and our lone milk cow. In the angle where the barbed wire pasture fence met the big roping and branding corral stood the threshing machine. Except for the tarp that covered the cylinder head and gearbox, it stood there exposed to the weather ten months of the year.

Its bright red paint had faded to a dull brick color. In winter the wind-whipped snow drifted deep around it, sifting into its innermost working parts. The spring rains seeped in also, starting pockets of rust and rot. Later still, the blazing summer sun took over and got in its dirty work of flaking the paint, warping the wood, drying up the grease and oil. But when threshing time came, it always worked. Crouching between the high conical grain stacks, gulping down the sheaves with a great roaring and shaking, sending out clouds of dust and chaff, it filled the big sacks with silvery oats and tawny wheat, and piled the clean yellow straw higher and higher. It was a major source of income to my father; for me it provided endless hours of entertainment and pleasure.

Standing bent-kneed on its towering back, I would—with loud cries and man-sized swear words—pretend to drive the four-horse team out through the lane gate and down the valley. Sometimes I would stand on the platform of the power unit, urging on my teams by means of a long whip borrowed without permission from the whipsocket of the buggy. Even on rainy days I could see it from the kitchen window, standing in its bleak surroundings and mud puddles, and I would dream of the excitement of the coming "thrashin'."

The next few weeks after Mr. Shaeffer's visit were mighty busy ones for everybody. My father had to get things in shape before he left on his threshing rounds. The last of the hay crop was cut and stacked, harness and threshing gear put into shape, the range cattle brought up and put on the home ranch. My mother had meat and vegetables to can, new school dresses to make for my sisters, and new shirts for me. Also, there was a horrible amount of housecleaning and clothes-washing to be done before my mother was satisfied. Horrible for me at any rate, for it seemed to me that the grownups spent all their waking hours dreaming up errands and jobs that only an eight-year-old boy could do.

I could hardly wait until the time came when I'd *really* be old enough to join the crew and maybe take Johnny Pfeiffer's place up there cracking the whip over the six teams, getting up each morning to water and feed them, making the last rounds at night. Then, digging a hole in the side of a newly made straw stack and wrapping my blanket around me, I would slide in and pull the straw snug about me and sleep warm and content, the thousand-acre prairie for a bedroom.

My father and his men often slept in this way in temperatures approaching zero, but they all agreed that getting up next morning was really tough. Some of the crew became known as "two-finger men." For them a morning washup consisted of gingerly dipping the first two fingers of each hand among the floating pieces of ice in the watering-trough and delicately dampening their eyes and lips. This was followed by a hasty wipe with the rough sleeve of a sheepskin coat. Then they were ready to head for the warm ranch house kitchen and a scalding cup of black coffee.

Early in September our new teacher arrived from the East

and was introduced to our beat-up log schoolhouse and its seven students, each in a different grade. A couple of days later, in the cold, ruddy light of early morning, the little cavalcade of threshers left for their first stand, where they would meet my father's partner, Carl, who would have spare teams and harnesses.

My father, standing easily on the careening separator, guided the four-horse team through the pasture gate and along the lane. Johnny Pfeiffer followed with one team pulling the power unit and another tailgating behind. The Studebaker wagon, loaded with bags of oats, bedrolls, and other miscellaneous gear, came next with Leo driving its team of four. Frank, astride his prized cow pony and leading Leo's saddle horse, brought up the rear.

By dark the rig would be set up at a ranch twenty miles to the east in the dry-land country, since the grain matured earlier in this high-bench land. The ranchers in the irrigated valleys to the west would be visited next. Then, late in October, my father would head toward home where he made his last stand to thresh his own grain crop. My mother came to dread the long absences these threshing trips necessitated. There was always the hired man to do the outdoor work and the schoolteacher and my teenage cousin Joe for company, and they could give some comfort and help in times of worry and trouble. But there was no substitute for my father's calm approach to a crisis and his competent manner of dealing with it. This was a good year, though, and the days drifted by, monotonous and uneventful. Once a heavy fall of snow held up operations long enough for him to return home for a few days to catch up on the more pressing chores and to show off the brand-new curly beard and sweeping mustache, both bright red, that he was growing as protection from the elements. These contrasted sharply with his blue eyes and jet black hair. The schoolteacher was visibly impressed and whispered soulfully to my mother one night as they stood by the sink doing dishes, "He's positively the handsomest man I ever saw."

My mother, flushing pink with pride, whispered back, "Yes, I know. But I never tell him so. He might get a swelled head."

October brought Indian summer, the lazy warm days carrying no hint of the biting cold and swirling snow soon to follow. Canada geese in long flickering Vs drifted across the sky, and their loud honking beat forlornly on our ears. "Where do they come from; where do they go?" we wondered. Each little pond and water-filled slough was littered with bright-feathered mallards and teal, snowy canvasbacks, and crested mergansers. Out among the grain stubble wandered flocks of prairie chickens, gleaning the grain left behind by the clattering binders and the lumbering grain wagons.

School settled to the usual dreary grind. The teacher turned out to be the no-nonsense-in-school type. You did your lessons and behaved properly or wound up standing in the corner or getting your knuckles rapped with the ruler, which seemed to be always in her hand and with which, I'm bound to say, she rapped us all with equal generosity.

But in the evenings, Grace, as we were soon calling her, was different. After supper we all crowded around the kitchen table under the yellow light from the nickel-plated coal-oil lamp, and she played simple pencil-and-paper games with us. Or she read to us from storybooks or the *Youth's Companion*. Sometimes we went on exciting shopping trips through the mail-order catalog. All this, of course, was when she was not entertaining the many unattached males who lived within riding distance of our ranch.

We watched the weather apprehensively, fearing the fine days might break up into one of our fierce snowstorms and bring with it a ruined grain crop. We were in the last week of the month when Frank arrived one evening with the welcome news that the rig and its crew would arrive by Friday night.

"I sure hope so," my mother told him. "This running the ranch by myself, together with worrying about the weather, has got me about worn out."

"Not too worn out to fix us some good eats, I hope," Frank said. "We ain't done so good the last couple of places."

My mother, her tiredness forgotten, reared up snorting fire. "Why those cheap—!" She broke off with an apologetic glance at the teacher and vigorously started firing out orders right and left. My cousin Joe came first.

"Joe, you see there's plenty of dry wood split up. I'll have a lot of baking to do."

"Iris, you better stay home from school tomorrow. Somebody'll have to watch the baby, and you'll have to go tell Uncle George to bring up that quarter of beef he's saving for us."

And, turning to Nettie, who had come to help with some sewing, "We'll have to let the sewing go for now. I'll need your help in the kitchen."

"Ma," I broke in, "can I—?"

She whirled around to me. "Whatever you want, it's *no*. I haven't got time for any of your monkeyshines. Just keep that woodbox full. You hear?"

"Yes, Ma," I answered meekly. I knew when she had a full head of steam and meant business.

It was full dark, and everyone had about given them up when I heard the eager whinny of a tired horse approaching his home barn. Running out on the porch, I could just make out the bulky silhouette of the separator at the top of the grade against the faint starlight of the Big Dipper.

"They're here! They're here!" I screamed into the kitchen and was off the porch like a shot, only to be stopped short by my mother's sharp voice from the doorway.

"You, Mick! Get back here and get your coat and cap." But on my way back out she added softly, "You want to catch your death?" and gave my shaggy hair a happy yank.

Accompanied by the musical clinking of iron wheels and horseshoes against the stony road, the caravan swung through the big gate.

"Whoa! Damn you all! Stand still a minute," my father spoke roughly to the horses. Then, more softly to my mother, "We're here, Peg. Boy, what a day! And are we starved! Didn't stop to eat. Seems like we've been on the road forever."

By the time the sun had cleared the prairie's rim that Saturday morning, everyone was hard at work. A team of horses dragged the thresher to its place between the grain stacks. The power unit was lined up on a spot carefully measured from the separator so that the sections of the drive shaft would come out just right when the two parts of the machine were joined. Johnny and Joe watered and fed the horses. Carl and my father uncovered the cylinder and set up the feeding tables ready to start. As usual I tried to be everywhere at once and succeeded in getting stepped on and bumped into continually. But all were in good humor, for the sky was clear and the sun was bright. It would be a good threshing day.

We hurried through our workday breakfast of hot oatmeal and cream, ham and eggs with fried potatoes, and platters of biscuit dough fried like pancakes, which my father liked so much he called them "dough gods." Just as we were finishing, the neighbors started to arrive—Uncle George and his hired man, each with a team and hay wagon, followed by Aunt Minnie and their kids in the spring wagon. From the opposite direction came my cousins George and Lily and their gang. Several other neighbors arrived in hay wagons and on horseback. Finally came Torval Johannsen, a middle-aged bachelor who was already a persistent admirer of the new teacher and who spoke a wild jargon of broken English. He drove in with thundering wagon and flying hair, and skidded to a halt in an obvious attempt to attract Grace's attention. Seeing her on the porch, he waved and grinned, showing his huge mouthful of tobacco-stained teeth. Then he turned to the rest of his audience and asked, "Vell, vy iss ve vaiting? Torval iss come."

"Hi! Hup!" Johnny's voice, competing with a series of loud whipcracks, announced the beginning of the day's work. Eight tons of horseflesh strained again the heavy sweeps, and the big cylinder began slowly, silently to revolve. Then, as the teams stepped up to a faster pace, its silence turned into a low growl, and from there it went up through the scale until it became a steady, singing roar. The sprocket wheels along the sides of the separator eased into motion and picked up speed, their chains tightening, glinting like water in the sun. Deep in the big machine's belly, the sieves began to shiver and shake, and the slats on the straw-carrier rattled and banged. The threshing machine had come to life. When the horses' pace and the whine of the cylinder satisfied my father's critical eye and ear, he nodded his head to the men on the grain stacks, and they began tossing the sheaves to the feeding tables. Here the bandcutters slashed the heavy twine, loosening the stalks that slid off and were gulped down by the ravenous monster.

I watched the whole operation intently, desperately wanting to have some part of it. True, my father had told me to keep the water pails full, and once Carl had allowed me to cut the hank of heavy cord to proper lengths for sewing the filled grain sacks. But mostly it was, "Keep away from the team, Mick, the off horse kicks." And, "Don't fool around that tumbling rod, boy. You'll get your overh'alls caught in a coupling and that'll be the end of you." Everyone was too busy with his own job to find one for me.

Dinner was a welcome break. The men washed up with much snorting and blowing at the wash bench outside the kitchen door, then combed their soaking wet hair with the metal comb hanging by a string beside the mirror nailed to the log wall. With a great deal of joking and scraping of chairs, the places around the kitchen table were quickly filled.

Feeding the "thrashin'" crew had a special significance in those times. A sort of county fair atmosphere prevailed, for it was an opportunity for the women to prove their reputations as cooks. Nothing fancy, just good, well-cooked food and lots of it. Of course, any cook with an ounce of pride belittled her efforts at least enough to ensure a few handsome compliments. My mother, who baked bread fit for the gods, always remarked as she passed the platter that "it hadn't raised just right this time," or that the mouth-watering coconut layer cake she was cutting had "fallen just a bit when one of the kids had slammed the kitchen door." Everyone knew that they were perfection itself— and so did she.

I was sure I would die of hunger before those at the first table were finished. It wasn't hard to persuade the younger men (also dying of hunger) to wait for the second table, for that was the one the schoolteacher presided over. As many of us older kids as there was room for also ate then. The women and smaller fry straggled along behind at a third and final table.

After dinner the men gathered in groups on the porch and down by the bunkhouse, discussing the price of wool and beef on the Chicago market and how much wheat and barley were bringing at the Conrad elevators. By one o'clock everyone was hard at work again.

But the festive atmosphere among the workers was gone now. A biting wind had blown up out of the north, and the sun had disappeared behind darkening clouds. The men cast apprehensive glances at the sky, making doleful predictions of snow before morning, and they increased their efforts. All too soon for me, the last load of grain went through the machine, the neighbors gathered up their families and effects, said their good-byes and left for their homes to batten down for the expected storm; and we were alone again. Another harvest was over.

After supper we all sat in the kitchen talking over the happenings of the day. My father had almost disappeared into a thick cloud of smoke from his favorite calabash pipe. Frank and Leo were puffing contentedly on fresh-rolled Bull Durham cigarettes. I had propositioned each of them hopefully for "just one puff," but my father's disapproving gaze discouraged that, and I retreated to my favorite perch on the freshly filled woodbox. I sat there in the shadows thinking about the day and how splendid it must be to be grown up and actually taking part in the "thrashin'." Finally, seeing the relaxed expression on my father's face, I blurted out, "Pa, next year can't I help *some* on the machine?"

He answered, a bit shortly, "You're too young, Mick. And it's too dangerous."

I persisted, close to tears. "But how'm I ever going to know how to run a thrashin' machine if you *never* let me do anything?"

His eyes softened, and he laid his pipe on the table beside him. "Come here, Mick," he said.

I slid off the woodbox and walked slowly over to him. His strong arm crooked around my shoulders.

"Look," he said, "just as soon as you're old enough I'll let you start doing things. Right now you're learning how. One way to learn anything is to watch. Someday you'll be the best damn thrashin' machine man in the whole state of Montana.

Only it's going to be a different kind of machine."

He reached up to the mantel shelf and pulled down a cata-log. Opening it, he pointed to a picture of a huge steam traction engine.

"That's what we'll have pretty soon instead of the old horsepower rig," he said proudly. "How'll you like to run that?"

I stared at the brightly colored picture in disbelief. It looked so huge, so complicated, so fascinating—almost too much to grasp.

"Gosh, Pa. You mean it?" Then I remembered. "How soon you going to get it? Won't I ever get to drive the horses?"

He laughed, "Don't worry, Mick. We haven't got it yet."

Later that night I went blissfully off to bed, already feeling my hand on the throttle as I steered the gleaming new rig across the prairie. I could picture myself sitting up there beneath its green metal canopy, its huge red wheels rolling along crushing down the heavy sod, its emblem of a bald eagle on top of the world painted boldly on its side, proclaiming to all that this was a genuine J. I. Case steam engine.

From Bow Bells to
Shining Mountains

IT WAS A RAW, WINDY DAY in late March. The schoolteacher, my sister, and I had bucked a strong west wind the mile home from school and were sitting in the warm kitchen, soaking up the delicious aroma of fresh-baked bread and cinnamon buns. My mother, after giving each of us a thick slice of hot bread ("doorstep," she called it) well topped with butter and wild strawberry jam, went to the window and looked out. When she gave a strangled cry, we all looked up. "My God, it's an Indian!" Then she added a little wildly, "Where's the baby?"

No matter what kind of disaster struck or what danger threatened, the first thing my mother always said was, "Where's the baby?" We made a rush for the window while she collected my younger sister and brother in a tight group around the baby buggy.

It was easy for me to tell that he was an Indian, all right, for he had dismounted on the right side of his horse instead of the left. And though he was standing behind his horse, I could see his hat showing above the horse's back and, underneath, his faded blue levis and moccasin-clad feet.

After tying his horse to a fence post, the Indian crawled through the strands of barbed wire and started rather unsteadily toward the house. My mother was scared of even sober Indians, and when she saw this drunken one staggering across the front yard, she almost collapsed. I added more fuel to her terror by announcing in a loud voice. "Hey! That's Crazy Dick!"

Among the Blackfeet on the reservation to the north of us, Crazy Dick had the reputation of being a bit unpredictable, especially after a few shots of bootleg whisky. He often went by the house on his way to town and spoke to my father or the hired men. But this was his first *call*.

By the time he reached the door and started to pound on it, my mother had pushed us kids and the baby carriage into a corner, fiercely on guard with her five-foot, ninety-pound frame. Luckily the teacher was a western girl, born and raised among the Flathead Indians over the mountains to the west, and had had some experience in handling them—drunk or sober.

She turned to my mother and whispered, "Be quiet and do just as I do."

My mother managed to nod her head.

Ruth went to the door and opened it wide. Crazy Dick strode without a word to the middle of the kitchen floor. He looked us all over, his face completely deadpan. Finally, stepping up to Ruth, he held out his hand. "How!" he said in a loud voice. Without hesitation she shook his hand and answered with a loud "How!" of her own. He then turned to my mother and held out his hand. "How!" he said again. My mother's indomitable cockney spirit stood her in good stead. Looking him in the eye, she grasped his outstretched hand and gave out with a strong "How!" that ended in a distinct squeak. After examining us openmouthed kids for a moment or two, he grunted a disgusted "Ugh!" turned on his heel, and stalked out of the door and across the yard. He had some trouble crawling through the fence and getting on his horse but finally managed it; then, heading north and urging the pony on with his waving hat and long, protracted whoops, he tore across the flats toward the reservation.

One thing about my mother, whenever she had one of these devastating experiences with our Montana natives—whether horses, cows, or people—she added it to her education of how to live better in this strange and unpredictable land. She had been born within sound of Bow Bells, the little church in the cockney district in London. "That makes me a cockney," she would say proudly. But her father, known as Montana Joe Paice because of his fanatical pride in his adopted land, would shout at her with gingery hair awry and blue eyes snapping, "Don't be proud of being any damn cockney! You live in Montana now!"

Her first few years in this country, living in Helena with her father, hadn't exactly prepared her for life on a cattle ranch, as she discovered when she married my father at the age of twenty-three. His ranch was on the prairie, close under the jagged peaks of the Continental Divide. These high mountains are usually well clad with snow fields, even in the heat of midsummer. When the sun shone on them in the early morning, they gleamed a dazzling white or rose. The Blackfeet revered them and many generations ago named them "Shining Mountains." Both my father and I shared some of this feeling, but my mother was repelled by their wildness and apprehensive of their dark forests and hidden ravines. She feared the dangerous animals that roamed those woods and the sudden floods that burst out of the canyons and down our peaceful valley. It took her years to accustom herself to these dangers and to the many unpredictable incidents of day-to-day living.

For instance, there was the simple matter of driving a horse. When my father climbed into a buggy, picked up the lines, and clucked to our most cantankerous driving horse, there was never any confusion in the animal's mind—he knew what to do. He took off at a smart trot through the gate and down the

lane. But when my mother drove the same horse, there must
have been something about her hesitant approach and her long
fluttering skirts that blew a fuse in him. In his fuzzy horse brain
he must have realized that this was his chance to be different.
And he usually was. Managing one horse was difficult, but for
her to drive a team was simply inviting disaster.

One afternoon my mother and I started to the Fisher ranch
for some setting eggs. We were driving Snort and Brownie, a
well broken but rather spirited team. The hitching-up went
well and my mother, her confidence at high peak, swung the
team through the gate and down the lane at a fast clip. A half-
grown calf had escaped from the pasture and was taking a nap in
the middle of the road and we were on him without warning.
"Look out! Look out!" my mother screamed at the calf, sawing
madly on the lines. The horses, confused by these strange com-
mands and startled by the appearance of a calf practically under
their feet, picked up speed and straddled him. Since cattle get
up hind end first, that's the part of him that got hit by the
heavy spring wagon. We couldn't see it, but there was quite a
commotion going on under us. A minute later, the horses under
control again, I looked back in time to see our terrified calf get
shakily to his feet and gallop for the safety of the barnyard.
That night at supper my father remarked slyly that he couldn't
understand how one of the calves had gotten all skinned up. My
mother snapped back that if he kept his stock behind the fences
where they belonged, strange things wouldn't happen to them.

My mother's extraordinary experiences with the natural
life included cows as well as horses and Indians. Mrs. Perkins,
our cross-eyed half-tamed milk cow, carried on a running battle
with my mother that lasted for years. Her brindled hide was as
tough as sole leather, and she could walk through a barbed wire
fence without a scratch—and often did—to raid the vegetable
garden. Beating her with a stick was of little use, so my mother
kept a pitchfork near the garden gate and jabbed her with some
success. She was also a smart cow and managed to find any un-
latched gate or unlocked door on the place. We had just gotten
home from town late one afternoon, and my mother was in the
kitchen, pulling out her long hat pins, when there was a loud

crash from the lean-to attached to the back of the cabin. It was a sort of storeroom and pantry where we kept bags of sugar, flour, and potatoes, and also, among other things, a dozen or so tin milkpans on a long shelf. These were probably what we heard falling to the floor. My mother opened the door, looked in, and, with a piercing scream, slammed it shut and shot home the bolt. My father, on his way to take the horse down to the stable, came back on the run.

My mother stood in the middle of the kitchen floor, pointing dramatically at the pantry door.

"Ed! There's a horrible animal in there!" she quavered.

"What kind of an animal?" he wanted to know.

"I don't know," she said. "It's huge and white, and it's got something on its head."

My father was used to her flights of fancy, but this really stumped him. Just then there was another loud thump, followed by rattlings from the scattered milkpans.

"Maybe it's a bear," I suggested hopefully.

"We'll soon see," he said confidently, but I noticed that he opened that door with extreme care. One quick look and he swung it wide, and there stood Mrs. Perkins, knee deep in the wreckage, calmly giving us a steady cross-eyed stare. The floor was littered with potatoes, milk pans, and crockery. The ripped hundred-pound flourbag dangled from one horn, its contents liberally dusting both the cow and the floor. A long dribble of foam ran down her chin.

"My God! Ed! She's gone mad!" my mother gasped.

And she wasn't quite reassured that Mrs. Perkins hadn't indeed gone mad until an hour later, when in the course of cleaning up the mess she discovered that the brindled glutton had eaten up her last three bars of Fels Naptha soap.

Not all these episodes ended on the funny side. Tragedy was always nearby—close enough that my mother often desperately wished to return to a more comfortable and secure way of life. She especially missed knowing that medical help was reasonably close by. One time my two-year-old brother fell into Sheep Creek during flood time and was carried quickly out of sight by the swift current. My father, working in a nearby field, heard our screams for help. He ran over and crashed through the willows lining the creek bank, finally pulling his son from the water a hundred yards downstream.

My father had worked in both gold mines and lumber camps so he had some knowledge of the rough first aid of those times. Sitting on a large rock by the side of the stream, he placed the little body across his knees, stomach down and head hanging low, and gently rocked him back and forth. A thin trickle of water dripped from the baby's mouth. My mother, kneeling helplessly by his side on the wet grass, was crying, "What will we do? It will take hours to get the doctor! Pat'll be dead long before then."

"We'll do something," my father said grimly, and just then Pat gave a faint gasp.

"Run up to the house and put some blankets on the oven," he commanded. "Heat some water and get the whisky." Then wrapping Pat in his coat, he hurried along behind.

As soon as he reached the kitchen, they stripped the baby of his sodden clothes and laid the small blue body in a warm blanket on the table. Somehow in their desperation they must have done the right things. An hour later Pat, warm and pink and well on the road to recovery, was tucked away in his crib. But it was many days before my mother recovered from the shock and terror of those few hours.

I used to think that Pat's long immersion in the muddy water of the creek had a definite effect on his character, that he had somehow absorbed some of the wild blizzards that formed the snow water, a little of the untamed mountain silt that roiled the raging stream, and a lot of the unpredictable and often devastating Montana climate. Pat not only attracted trouble, he was extremely good at inventing it.

At the age of five he took his three-year-old brother Joe (nicknamed the "Honey Boy") egg hunting. We let our chickens run loose, and of course they laid eggs all over the place. We were continually looking for their nests under brush piles, in the haystacks, and throughout the barns. Pat and the Honey Boy finally reached the horse barn in their search for eggs, and in the first stall, as they entered, was a black mare named Maud.

"Don't go near the horse barn today," my father had said at breakfast, "Maud's in there, and she's a kicker. You hear?"

To Pat, the word *don't* was a challenge. Thus, with his small brother in tow, he entered the door and passed behind the stall. Startled, Maud let fly with both feet and struck Joe alongside the head, tumbling him across the barn and against the log wall. Badly frightened and incensed at the mare, Pat threw his hat full of eggs at her and dashed off to the house. Finding the screen door hooked, he pounded on it frantically as he screamed, "Mamma! Mamma! Come quick. Old Maud's kicked the Honey Boy and he's dead!"

Getting kicked by a horse often resulted in tragedy, and my mother dashed out to the stable fearing the worst. She found Joe lying in a crumpled heap in the straw, and in the stall was Maud standing with ears back and feet ready, her black coat plastered with broken eggs.

It was a school day, and my father and the hired man were building a line fence on the far side of the ranch leaving my mother alone. But somehow she managed, and by the time we came home from school, the Honey Boy had gotten his senses back, but my mother looked as if she would never laugh again.

She did, of course. As the days and months and years went by, she gradually adapted herself to things as she found them. A person of boundless energy, she always found time for interests other than the usual housework. She especially enjoyed raising chickens, much to my father's disgust. Like all Montana ranchers, he never had the interest or time to build a proper chicken house and just got mad whenever he found his wagons and farm machinery well-sprinkled with chicken droppings.

She was also an enthusiastic gardener, but after some discouraging experiences of trying to grow flowers and grass in our mulish climate, she finally concentrated on a vegetable garden, of which she was justifiably proud. With some of us helping, she worked in it nearly every evening after supper, her long dress hiked up to her knees, gum boots on her feet, and an old felt hat of my father's on her head. Since she alternated between pulling weeds and slapping mosquitoes, her face would gradually become tinted weed-green and stippled with mud. We always stopped work early enough to stand around, straightening kinks out of aching backs and admiring the long, lush rows of peas and beans, the frilly carrot tops, and the deep red of future beet greens. Each spring she set a goal—green peas and new potatoes for the Fourth of July dinner.

One of the most familiar sounds to greet our ears when we arrived home from school was the hum of her sewing machine. It was usually going at top speed, her feet a blur on the treadle, the cloth running like quicksilver under the needle. In minutes she would have Iris standing on a chair, and mumbling through a mouthful of pins, she would make final adjustments on a dress. Or she would be debating with the teacher, half hidden among the many yards of unfinished dress, about the length of the hem, the hang of a flounce, or the number of ruffles to be added to the skirt. About five o'clock my mother would reluctantly fold up the unfinished garments and push the machine into its corner. Soon the men would be in for dinner. The kitchen fire was energetically stoked up and the teakettle filled, accompanied by the staccato clanking of the pitcher pump. Then, musing happily on her latest dress creation, she rattled and banged her way through the preparations for the evening meal.

With the arrival of the teacher each new school year, my mother started her campaign to arrange a marriage between the unsuspecting girl and one of our neighboring bachelors. She spent hours conspiring with other interested matrons, arranging parties, and even stooping to tip off some favored suitor on ways to improve his chances. Though the results were usually disappointing, she never tired of her matchmaking role.

Opportunities for fun and entertainment were so scarce that we seldom missed a school dance, a box social, a picnic, or a card party. I especially enjoyed the dances. Some of the girls could chord the pump organ, there was an old-timer that scraped a mean fiddle, and my cousins took turns playing the mouth organ and beating out time with a high-heeled boot. I could sit all night watching the dancers go skipping through sets of the Virginia reel, or the intricate figures of the schottische, or just an old-fashioned hoe down, the boys swinging the girls 'til their feet left the floor. Occasionally, my mother or one of the older girls would drag me through the mysteries of a Paul Jones, after which I would retire to my seat beside the organ, flushed and happy and wishing the night would never end. But a couple of hours past midnight our homespun orchestra would strike up "Home Sweet Home" for the last whirling pump-handle waltz, and I would see my mother, eyes sparkling and long ruffled skirts flying, dancing that last dance as if she too wished it were the first.

Although my mother was of a naturally cheerful and optimistic disposition, she had so many brushes with near tragedy, which often struck with nerve-shattering suddenness, that she was always braced for the worst.

One day when I went for the cows with an older cousin, "Tots," we came across a large bed of wild sweetpeas. With his encouragement I ate heartily of the ripened peas and became violently sick in minutes. My badly frightened cousin staggered home with me in his arms. Laying me on the grass near the door, he hurried into the house to confess to my mother what had happened. She came running out to find me just coming out of a convulsion, and though terror-sticken, she managed to pour a cup of mustard and water down my throat. I immediately threw up, and by the time my father came running up from the corral, the worst was over. We later learned that these peas were extremely poisonous. Her prompt and correct action probably saved my life.

I was pretty sick that night and spent the next day in bed, being waited on by everybody and having a grand time. I even had tea and saltine crackers at dinner time instead of the regular ranch fare. But when my father came in late in the afternoon, asking for an early supper because he had to go to town to have a mowing machine casting welded, I got well fast. I came out of the bedroom half dressed, claiming I felt fine and couldn't I go to town with him?

My mother, still harboring a desire to wring my neck because I was so dumb as to eat those poisonous peas, put her foot down. "After the scare that kid gave me last night," she said, "he isn't going to get out of my sight for a month."

Then she added. "Why don't you take Iris with you? She needs a change once in a while too! Tots can stay with me."

But my father said Tots was supposed to go to town and get a new pair of shoes. My mother was in a reckless mood. "That's all right with me," she said grandly. "After he let Mick eat that stuff last night, I wouldn't trust him with a dead horse. I'd rather be alone. At least we won't go looking for trouble."

After supper my father, with Tots and Iris beside him, drove off, rashly promising to be home by dark "if possible."

When the team and wagon had crawled up the hillside and disappeared over its crest, I climbed down off the gate and went up to the house, only to be handed a dishtowel and invited to wipe the dishes—which I did with poor grace. Now that we were alone, my mother, a little nervous but not wanting to show it, invented a lot of small jobs to keep us busy. I claimed that I was still "kind'a sick," but it didn't work, and dusk found us still pulling weeds in the vegetable garden. It got dark fast, with a blanket of clouds creeping from behind the mountains and over the house and on across the prairie to the east.

"I wish your father would come," she said. "Let's go in and light the lamp."

She bustled around getting Lucy, Pat, and the baby settled for the night, but she didn't say anything about my going to bed as she usually did about dark.

We got out the cards and played several games of Old Maid, the only card game I knew. Finally, she stopped and sat for a few moments looking alternately from the black window panes to the round, nickel-plated alarm clock on the shelf. It was eleven o'clock, and they should have been home by now. She got up and went over to the clock, wound it with her usual vigorous twists, gave it a few healthy shakes, and set it back on the shelf. "Thought maybe it had stopped," she said.

It was only a few minutes later that we heard the faint, faraway wailing. We looked at each other. "Coyotes?" I ventured. But she shook her head, growing more rigid in her chair. "Indians!" she whispered. Suddenly the confused whooping and wailing, accompanied by pounding hoof-beats and metallic rattlings, grew much louder. They were over the hill and descending into the valley.

"The light!" she exclaimed and jumped to her feet and blew out the lamp. Then she slammed the front door and shot the bolt, calling for me to shut the back door and hurry—which I did. We stood rooted to the floor, listening intently.

"They've turned into our lane," my mother suddenly gasped. "Come help me!"

I could hear something being dragged along the floor as I stumbled across the pitch-black kitchen. She was trying to push the table across the front door. I helped her drag it; then we piled all the kitchen chairs on top. We remembered the back door and with superhuman effort managed to shove the sideboard in front of it, paying no attention to the crash of broken pottery as the cups and plates tipped to the floor. Then clutching me by the arm, she raced to the bedroom where the babies were, and shut and locked the door.

Just then the racket stopped outside the front door. In the sudden quiet I whispered, "Maybe they're going to burn the house down." Old man Alcorn had told me about the Indian raids of thirty years ago, and I knew all the procedures. Before she could answer, someone tried to open the door, and, finding it locked, pounded on the panel. She clutched me convulsively and hissed into my ear, "*Quiet!*"

Pictures of painted Indians brandishing tomahawks and scalping knives rushed through my mind. My heart pounded like mad, and I could hear my mother's breath coming in short, convulsive gasps. Our ears were straining for the next move of the Indians, when gradually I became aware of a familiar sound.

"Peg! Peg!"

It was my father's voice. "Peg! Open up, Peg! What's the matter?"

We tiptoed from the bedroom and cautiously approached the door. Even then she wasn't entirely convinced. "Ed! Are you sure that's you?" she asked.

"Of course, I'm sure it's me," he said with considerable amazement. "Who did you think it was? Chief Four Horns?"

Later, when the lamps were lit and the furniture was back

in place, my mother's emotions had gone from terror, to relief, then back to pleasure, and on up to justifiable anger. "How could you come home yelling and racing the horses like that in the middle of the night?" she demanded fiercely. My father was earnestly trying to defend himself. "We weren't yelling! We were singing "White Wings."

No man west of the Mississippi was a worse singer than my father. And when he got going on "White Wings," no one ever sang louder.

My mother shook her head hopelessly and remarked to the world in general, "Another scare like this will be the end of me."

But it was not this kind of a scare that nearly ended her. It was a serious operation and only the skill of Dr. Powers, a wonderful country doctor in Conrad, some forty miles to the east, saved her life.

The night my father brought her home from the hospital, where she had been for six long weeks, everyone had pitched in, and the house was spotless. We kids had stood inspection by the schoolteacher and were sitting around, for once all clean at the same time. Even Nolan, the hired man, had gone to town for a haircut and a new bright-red flannel shirt. Mrs. Howe, our temporary housekeeper, had been cooking and baking most of the day, and was now fluttering around inspecting pies in the oven and lifting potlids to check what was underneath, but without any zip or authority. That's what I had been missing these long weeks. No one to remind me sharply that the woodbox was empty or to give me a hug and a cookie when I piled in the last armful of fragrant stovewood. The sewing machine in the corner had been silent, and the evening chatter around the big oil lamp quiet and listless. I had spent more and more time sitting gloomily on the woodbox counting the days until my mother came home.

Peering through the gathering dusk of the fall evening, I saw the buggy turn into the lane and head briskly for the house.

"They're here! They're here!" I screamed and, followed by the whole gang of yelling kids and a barking dog, raced down the path and across the bridge. After hugs and kisses all around, my father ordered us back to the house. "You'll have to take it easy. Your mother's tired," he said. But she shook her head and led us back to the house and through the kitchen door. There she stopped, sniffed the fresh-baked bread and mince pie, looked slowly around at the bright kitchen and our happy faces. Turning to my father, she exclaimed in an awed voice, "I would never have believed that this godforsaken ranch could be so beautiful."

A Trip to Town

A TRIP TO TOWN, ten miles away, was a real event in our lives. Sometimes the excitement began even before we started out. One time we were all ready to start when my younger sister, dressed in all her Sears-Roebuck finery, walked straight off the edge of the bridge across our creek into four feet of water. My father pulled her out and shook her back to her senses; I rescued her hat as it floated downstream; and my mother dragged her, howling, back to the house to repair the damage.

The earliest of these offside events that I remember hearing about took place when I was about three years old. It involved my mother and Bugeater, an ex-cow pony, who was generally steady and reliable but was given to occasional lapses from conformity. He was the source of the abiding distrust my mother had for all driving horses. It was years before she became convinced that you pulled—not pushed—on the lines to make a horse go ahead.

On this particular day, when my father was away with his threshing rig, my mother decided to drive to town. While we dressed, the hired man hitched Bugeater to the light buggy and tied him to the hitching post outside the cabin door, not far from the small mountain of split stovewood that always stood by the corner of the house. I can recall now the sense of anticipation I felt as my sister and I settled into the seat and watched my mother pick up the lines and give Bugeater a gentle slap with them across his rear. The result was instantaneous. Bugeater spied the woodpile behind him. Never having climbed a woodpile, the idea apparently fascinated him. He took off at a queer kind of backward gallop, and in no time at all we hit full tilt and stopped, the buggy perched rakishly half way up the woodpile. The passengers had but one thought—abandon ship! We must have all jumped for the same spot at the same time, for we landed in a heap on the ground. Bugeater stopped dead still and looked back over his shoulder at us with what my mother always insisted was a smirk. We sorted ourselves out, discovered no damage to ourselves or the wagon, and, after Mother had vented her cockney wrath on the culprit, proceeded to climb a bit hesitantly back into the buggy. Bugeater, chastened either by the unexpected resistance of the woodpile or by my mother's tongue-lashing, carried us to town and back as sedately as a country parson conducting a prayer meeting.

Vehicles of transportation in those days might be anything from a four-horse team and lumber wagon to a high-speed cow pony hitched between the shafts of a light buggy. And the roads were hardly deserving of the name. Occasionally, where a road came down a hillside into a valley, there was some rough grading, and streams sometimes sported a crude bridge, though most were forded at a shallow spot. Many of the roads were never laid out or constructed at all; they just happened. Ranchers would drive back and forth to town following the path of least resistance, and after a while these well-worn ruts across the prairie became known as "roads."

Our horses came in a variety of colors and sizes, and a wide range of talents. The workhorses, docile and slow, were used when the load was heavy. The saddle ponies were strictly for riding and would kick apart or run away with anything on wheels. A fast but gentle driving horse was hard to come by and was greatly prized, especially by the women. Then there were the jokers—emotional, stubborn, cantankerous, unpredictable beasts.

Ordinarily, my father drove on our trips to town, and the whole family went along, for these were big events—breaks in the long stretch of lonely days on the prairie. The trips, of course, were subject to weather conditions. Three or four hours in an open wagon during a driving rainstorm or a blizzard could pretty well dampen your enthusiasm for any kind of a trip. But even if the day was clear and balmy when we started, there was no knowing what it would be like when we were ready to come home. Our part of Montana was known for its sudden shifts in weather, sometimes because of the abrupt thaws brought in on the chinook winds from the coast, sometimes because of icy gales from the high mountains that could turn the air bitterly cold as suddenly as a chinook could warm it.

Just getting ready for a trip could be a frustrating and time-consuming experience. It usually fell to me to take a halter, walk a quarter of a mile to a 160-acre pasture lot, and try to catch a half-wild horse that didn't want to be caught. The minute even a dumb horse saw me stalking him with a halter, he grew suspicious and kept a clean hundred feet between us. The smart ones were warier. Eventually, with a pan of oats and a mouth full of sweet talk, I could manage to seduce the critter I was after; but it took a lot of perseverance, and the horse always seemed to enjoy the pastime more than I. Once I got the halter on him, however, he invariably became so amiable that he would step all over my feet and slobber down my neck. Then I would have to go back into the house and change my shirt.

My father, in the meantime, was—with many an "ouch" and "damn"—subjecting his week's growth of whiskers to his well-stropped (but seldom really sharp) straight razor and forcing his unwilling limbs into his one and only suit—dark green and decidedly tight, as I remember it. My mother and my oldest

sister, Iris, after scrubbing and dressing the squealing, squirm-
ing small fry and perching them on separate chairs at a safe distance from one another, would threaten dire punishments if
they moved a muscle or in any way got a speck of dirt on their
clean clothes or shining faces. Then they began their own special ritual of "getting ready." First, my mother lit an oil lamp
and slipped the curling iron down into the chimney above the
flame to heat while she put on and laced up her long, black
town shoes. I liked to watch her take the curling iron out, lick
one finger and touch it to see if it hissed, wind her straight red
strands of hair around it, hold it steaming (or smoking) for a
moment, then pull it away from the little corkscrew spiral it had
made. When she had a row of these curls across her forehead
and another row below the bun in back, she combed them into
an airy fringe. She would never dream of going to town without
those curls. It would be like going half dressed, she often declared. After a light dusting with rice powder, she donned a
wasp-waisted dress with a high collar and leg-of-mutton sleeves,
and anchored her broad-brimmed hat with foot-long, silver-
headed pins. Iris, in rag-curled ringlets and starched white dress,
stood stoically while my mother went through the inevitable
final pulls and tugs of adjustment. Then, at last, we were about
ready to go. There was still the stowing away of anywhere from
two to six kids in the wagon, however, and this often led to some
friction. But after my mother had distributed a few healthy wal-
lops to assorted small rears, things quieted down, and we were
on our way.

To me, the ride never seemed long because there was so
much to see. I liked to listen to the wailing call of the curlews
and watch them wheeling above the prairie grass. Cries of excitement and much pointing of fingers accompanied the occasional sight of a great bald eagle soaring in from the mile-high
mountains to the west. Here and there a coyote would be seen
trotting across a distant coulee. And there were nearly always
jackrabbits and prairie dogs in sight somewhere. Stray range
cattle and horses, grazing at will, were carefully scrutinized for
brand markings and physical condition. In spring and summer,
the prairie grasses and buckbrush grew green and thick, well

sprinkled with purple crocuses and the waxy golden blossoms of
the prickly pear. Meadowlarks whistled from fence posts, and
sometimes wild ducks and Canada geese flew over, heading
north for their nesting grounds. Now and then, a small flock of
prairie chickens would scuttle across the road in front of us.
The only trees we saw were the lines of willows and cottonwoods and chokecherries along the stream beds. The horses trotted leisurely along, the steel rims of the wheels clinking against
the stones, until the last turn came in the road, and there was
the big bridge and across it the town.

Main Street was simply a wide space of trampled dirt between two rows of buildings. During the spring and fall rains it
was a bottomless quagmire, crossed on foot only in cases of extreme necessity. During the summer the dust lay ankle deep,
lifted into whirling dust devils by stray gusts of wind and into
huge clouds by any passing vehicle. Another street crossed this
one, forming a T. We drove up the base of the T, passing four
saloons, a livery stable, blacksmith shop, and several other
buildings, then stopped in front of Harris Brothers' General
Store. We scrambled down from the wagon and trooped into
the store, where all our purchases were made—from twenty-
penny nails and gum boots to flour, dress patterns and fabrics,
dishes, shoes for us kids and—for the treat of the day—some bars
of Hershey's chocolate. While my father and mother were buying
supplies, I would walk around the store smelling the strange
smells of pickle barrels, kerosene, and new cloth, and would
look at all the wonders on the shelves waiting to be purchased.
Friends and neighbors came in, greeting each other, exchanging
news and gossip, talking about the next box-social and dance. In
one corner was the post office, where we got our own mail and
that of all the ranchers we would pass on the way home. This
was the only R.F.D. there was in those days, and when the
weather was so bad that no one was driving to town, several
weeks went by when no one got any mail at all.

Most fascinating of all to me were the Indians. In summer,
they squatted on their heels on the store porch with their backs
to the wall. In winter, they sat around the big sheet-iron stove.
They were dressed in moccasins, faded levis, heavy wool

blankets (usually army issue) over their shoulders, and wide-
brimmed, high-crowned black felt hats. Their faces were expres-
sionless, and they almost never spoke; but if I watched carefully, I would see their hands making quick, furtive movements
—the universal sign language of the Plains Indians. They also
gave off a most penetrating odor, which we called "Indian
smell"—probably a combination of unwashed bodies and the
rancid animal fat with which they smeared themselves. These
were the older, "blanket" Indians. The younger ones hung
around the saloons, and though it was unlawful to sell them
whisky, by nightfall they usually managed to get a few drinks.
They would climb on their ponies and with loud whoops and
yells race up and down the street a couple of times, then clatter
across the bridge and head for the Blackfoot reservation. How
the older Indians got to town or where they went when the
store closed up at night, I never knew.

One of the most interesting places in town for me was the
blacksmith shop. Pete St. Denis, the blacksmith, was a friend of
the family, and his son Louis and I were good friends. I would
often hang around there whether our own horses and wagon
needed attention or not. Louis and I sometimes helped turn the
crank on the forge blower and watched the brilliant sparks and
blue and red flames roar above the heater and on up the chimney, as the black iron horseshoe the smith was working on
turned cherry red. We raced around, got underfoot, and asked
silly questions, but Pete never minded. The delicious mixture
of smells—soft-coal smoke from the forge, hot iron, burnt hoof,
and horse sweat—was sweet to my young and uncultured nose,
and it was always hard to tear myself away. But there were other
places I liked to go, too.

One was the livery stable. This was supposed to be off lim-
its for me since it was the hangout of the less savory elements of
the town; but I went there, nevertheless. Often, there was a
drunk sleeping in the hay or a fight to watch behind the stable;
and there was always the rough talk of the stable hands and
hangers-on. And there was the owner's son, who was my age and
a real tough kid. We had fun together for a while, sometimes
swimming in the creek back of the stable or fooling around the

horses in the corral and in their stalls. But we nearly always wound up having a fight, and when I met up with my parents later in the afternoon, cut and bruised with torn, dirty clothes, there was never much doubt in their minds where I had been. By then, though, they were usually in a hurry to get started for home, and the punishment I had coming was often postponed or, better yet, forgotten altogether.

One Saturday late in May of the year when I was nine or ten, my father and the schoolteacher and I left for town in a rainstorm. Since the teacher had to catch the stage and then the train that would take her "back East" where she lived, we couldn't wait for a good day. By late afternoon the rain had become a downpour; it was decided that we would stay overnight with the blacksmith's family. We had a fine time playing games, eating fudge, looking at the latest stereopticon slides, and listening to the new Edison talking machine with the big tin horn, which only the oldest daughter was allowed to touch. The shiny black cylinder was carefully taken from its round cardboard box and fitted onto the machine. The crank was twisted round and round, and the switch turned on. Out came the magic words, preceded always by the announcement, "This is an Edison record." About bedtime, someone looked out the window and announced that the rain had turned to snow.

Next morning, we looked out upon a wild and unbelievable world. The wind must have built up during the night, for the prairie and surrounding mountains and even the nearby buildings had disappeared in a whirling, smothering mass of flying snow. Drifts were already waist-deep and had started to creep over the fences and up the side of the buildings. By noon it was plain that the storm was far from spent but we decided to try to get home, for my mother and an adolescent nephew were alone on the ranch, trying to supply the fires with wood, feed the stock, and care for five small children.

After a hearty noon meal, we hitched Snort and Brownie, our light traveling team, to the wagon. The wagon bottom was filled with hay and covered with horseblankets to make a bed for me—not for sleeping but as protection against the storm. My father, in a borrowed buffalo coat, his cattleman's hat tied on with a heavy wool-scarf, climbed up on the wagon seat and headed the horses toward home—directly into the teeth of the wind.

At first the going wasn't too bad. The buildings in town and the trees along the creek just outside gave some protection, but once we crossed the bridge and came out onto the open prairie, the wind had a full sweep at us. Horses—indeed all animals—hate to travel into the wind. They tend to drift continually downwind, so just keeping them headed right was no mean job. Every buffalo wallow had drifted full, and when the team floundered into one of these six-foot holes, they frantically kicked and struggled to regain their footing. Here my father's knowledge of how to handle horses probably saved our lives, for once lost or unable to go on, we could easily have frozen to death. There was no help in the deserted, snow-filled world of the open prairie. My father would talk softly to the frightened animals, soothing them, holding their heads down so they would stay still until they had quieted. I climbed out and helped when I could, unhooking a tangled trace, unsnapping a neckyoke so a horse could get up, or straightening out the lines. After getting the horses on their feet and ready to go on—which often took half an hour or more of precious daylight each time—I would stomp off the snow the best I could and crawl back into the hay beneath the blanket.

Too soon the short afternoon was gone, and the blinding snow-filled darkness brought renewed fears of becoming hopelessly lost. After each struggle in the smothering snowdrifts, we headed the horses again into the wind, and after hours of constant urging and moving at a snail's pace, we came at last to our line fence. Here we turned cross-wind and plowed our way toward the house. Even here we had to proceed with utmost care. If we lost sight of the fence, we would be as thoroughly lost as we would have been a hundred miles from home. So my father walked within touch of the barbed wire strands, leading the team. About midnight, we reached the big pole swing-gate and made out the faint gleam of the house lights across the creek. No castle in Spain ever looked as beautiful as that old log house did to us. No glimpse of Heaven could equal the sight of the happy faces of the family and the warmth of the big lamp-lit kitchen with its huge black range, red-hot in spots, and the pitchpine fire roaring deep in its innards.

Later, reveling in the luxury of the fierce heat from the fire, our stomachs filled with beef stew and fresh-baked bread, we told and retold the story of our trip to town. My mother remarked that one never knew what might happen when starting out on a trip to town. She reminded us of the time when we were coming home in a violent thunderstorm and lightning struck her umbrella, scaring the wits out of all of us, including the horses. "I almost had a runaway team on my hands," she said. "But you know, I think they were too scared to run!" My cousin chimed in then about the time the team he and his brother Frank were driving *had* run away, almost killing them both when the horses chose opposite sides of a tree to run around.

Flooded with contentment and half asleep, I listened to the comfortable talk, while outside the wind tore and shrieked around the eaves and occasionally blasted down the chimney, rattling the stove lids and blowing puffs of smoke into the room.

Cowboys and Hired Hands

IT WAS A LATE AFTERNOON toward the end of January, and the sun was shining brightly, filling the kitchen with warmth and cheer. But the thermometer hanging in a sheltered angle of the porch read twelve degrees below zero. The high mountains to the west, instead of sheltering us, merely added speed to the bitter wind that slid down their steep slopes and raced across the prairie, starting up whirling geysers of powder-dry snow. These snow geysers wandered downwind and settled on the growing snowbanks along the valley's rim and down among the willows that lined the creek's bank.

It was a good day to be inside. My father was out in the barn starting his evening chores. My mother, trapped between trying to finish a dress she was making and getting supper started on time, was pedaling the old Singer with continuous bursts of frantic stitching. My sisters were cutting valentines from old wallpaper catalogs at the kitchen table, and Miss Reynolds, our teacher, sat opposite them, writing letters.

My mother had banished me to the pantry for fighting with my sisters, and I sat on a chair by the window working steadily at opening a peephole in the frosted window pane. I was a little dizzy from my steady blowing by the time I had melted a spot in the ice large enough to see out clearly. The road down the lane had disappeared under the drifting snow, and the only clue to its whereabouts was the two parallel barbed wire fences that struggled across the flats and buried themselves under the snowbanks along the hillsides. As I watched, three horsemen traveling Indian file appeared out of the flying snow and turned into the lane. The men sat stiffly, their heads bent to the wind, while the horses, tinted silver by the hoarfrost on their long coats, plodded slowly along, starting long streamers of snow streaking downwind.

"Three horseback riders coming down the lane," I called out.

The pen and scissors dropped to the table with a clatter, and the sewing jerked to a stop in midstitch as everyone crowded up for a look. My mother opened the door wide enough to stick her head out and take a quick look, then, with a shiver, she slammed it shut.

"It's Frank," she said. "Bringing home a couple of grub-line riders, I'll bet."

Frank, my twenty-year-old cousin, was working for us that winter. He had gone into town early that morning for supplies and mail. He was good-looking, an expert rider and roper, and always wore high-heeled boots and a tan Stetson hat. He would also let me sneak an occasional puff from his cigarette when he thought neither my father nor my mother would notice. He was my hero!

My mother tried to sound grumpy, but a distinct note of pleasure crept into her voice, for it was the lonesome time of the year, and almost any kind of company was a welcome break in the winter's monotony.

Because of our isolation from the outside world as well as from our neighbors, we were thrown into close contact with a succession of cowboys, schoolteachers, hired hands, "crazy sheepherders," and even wandering Blackfoot Indians. These cow-

boys and hired hands were not the old frontier-type cowpunch-
ers that spent all their time working cattle, following the
roundups, packing a six-gun on their hips, and shooting up the
saloons on a drunken spree, but most of them were good riders,
ropers, and cattlemen. Many also retained much of the old glamour in their dress and talk and payday celebrations in town.
Some were dull and soon forgotten, but many were free, independent characters who became good friends and even, for a
time, almost part of the family. I especially liked the happy,
carefree grub-line riders.

Between the end of the fall threshing and the start of the
spring plowing, outside work on the ranches came pretty much
to a standstill, which left many of the young men jobless. Some
of them were "proving up" on their own homesteads and spent
the winter months working on them. The others were by nature
far from thrifty and usually started their long lay-off virtually
penniless. In order to survive the long winter, they made the
rounds of the ranches, usually visiting alone, but sometimes in
pairs. This was called "riding the grub-line." Most of the ranchers understood the situation and made these wandering guests
welcome. However, after a week or ten days, even the most
motherly of ranch wives, eyeing her fast-dwindling supply of
home-canned vegetables and corned beef, would more or less
delicately suggest that the visit was over.

"I'm going down to the bunkhouse," I told my mother, as I
climbed into my felt boots and sheep-lined coat and made a
dash for the door.

"Tell them supper will be ready in an hour," she called
after me, as I skidded down the icy path and across the footbridge.

My father was already in the old cabin and had stoked up
the sheet-iron chunk stove with pine knots. By the time it had
broken out in cherry-red spots along its black sides, the riders
came crowding in, stamping their numb feet on the floor and
groaning loudly when the blood began recirculating in their
half-frozen feet and hands. Later, the two riders, Cliff and Gus,
brought in their bedrolls and tossed them on the extra bunks
while Frank handed over to my father the grain sack of supplies

and a large bundle of mail.

"Supper'll be ready by the time you've stabled your horses and washed up," he told them as he started for the house, anxious to look over the three-week collection of letters and papers.

Supper was a great success. My mother had delayed it long enough to curl her red hair and dust rice powder lightly on her face. Our young teacher, decked out in her next-to-best dress and well sprinkled with cologne, looked beautiful and smelled delicious. She seemed to have pretty much the same effect on the three young men sitting opposite her as she had on me. Frank, comfortable and at home, reported the latest news and gossip from Dupuyer between mouthfuls; but Gus and Cliff, their faces reddened from the long ride in the biting wind, their hair combed soaking wet and plastered down, sat tongue-tied with their eyes glued to their plates except for an occasional self-conscious glance at the teacher's face.

After supper the three men hovered around the cooking range, getting in the way of my mother, who was busy with her evening chores, until in exasperation she ordered them to sit down somewhere or else go back to the bunkhouse.

"Gosh, Aunt Peggy," Frank protested, winking at the schoolteacher, "this fire feels so good yet. We're still half frozen from that ride. I don't think I'll ever get really warm again."

"No wonder," my father snorted from behind his paper. "Riding out in this weather in those damn cowboy hats and boots."

"Shucks," Frank said, "I'm saving felt boots and ear-lapper caps for my old age."

"Besides," Cliff admitted sheepishly, "we didn't exactly ride all the way. We walked and led the horses most of the time. After riding about ten minutes in that wind, the snow felt mighty warm on our feet."

Later, the dishes washed and put away and the little kids tucked into bed, my mother and Iris set out on a window-shopping tour of the new Sears-Roebuck catalog. The teacher and the three cowboys were having a noisy game of Pedro at one end of the kitchen table. From my seat on the woodbox, I watched them with all the self-pity of an ignored eight-year-old. The

men, now completely thawed out both physically and emotion-
ally, were busily competing for the teacher's smiles. And she,
floating in a young lady's seventh heaven (three ardent admir-
ers all to herself), charmed them all equally and without favor.
I enviously turned my eyes away from the card game and looked
out at the cold, white moon that hung over Split Mountain and
listened to the swish of wind-driven snow as it swirled around
the corner of the house. Won't it be wonderful, I thought, when
I grow up and can wear cowboy boots whenever I want, and
have my own horse and saddle, and ride the grub-line through
the long winter months?

Almost everything the cowboys did around the ranch fascinated me, and I was always on their heels. When Frank stood in
the corral, all the horses milling around him, and whirled his
lariat to catch his half-wild horse, I was usually on the fence
watching. When I knew the men were due with a bunch of
calves for branding, I spent half the day watching for the cloud
of dust and listening for the bawling of the cattle in the distance so that I could be there to open the gate when they arrived. When a young horse was to be harness-broken or when
someone rode a bucker on a Sunday afternoon just for the sport
of it, I was all the while being jerked back out of danger. I
couldn't get close enough, it seemed. And when they were at the
dances, all togged up in polished boots and plastered-down hair,
I still thought I could follow them around—joining them out
behind the schoolhouse for a sneak drink and a shady story. But
I never made it past my mother's watchful eye. Best of all, I
liked to sit down in the bunkhouse with them while they
hashed over the day's happenings or talked with sly winks and
raised eyebrows about their last trip to town, the Saturday night
dance, the poker games at the saloon, and their last visit to that
strange "unmentionable" house.

With the exception of my young cousins and a few of the
neighbors who often worked for us and were real cowboys, we
had to rely on drifters and transients for help. These hired
hands could be full of surprises both good and bad.

Old Man Moon was one of the drifters. Tall and thin, with
his sparse hair and grey mustache, he seemed to me much older

than his actual years. I was rather in awe of him because even at work he wore a black cutaway coat and derby hat. He also had a glass eye, which he occasionaly removed and put on a shelf in the bunkhouse. My mother would throw a fit whenever he appeared at mealtime with a gaping hole in his face. "Mr. Moon," she would say very formally, but with strong feeling "go get your eye and put it in, or else pack your suitcase and head for town!" He would go meekly back to the cabin and get his eye but a few days later would forget again. He was a little off-center about religion and spent countless hours trying to rescue my cousins and me from eternal damnation—a futile and hopeless hobby, I might add. He also liked to concoct home remedies. One of his favorite and most regularly used specialties was a cough medicine made from juniper berry juice and Gordon's gin.

He seemed to migrate with the birds. For a number of years he appeared every summer and stayed for a few weeks or months. But one fall he disappeared for good.

Then there was Joe Blum, a hired man my father brought home from town one day. He was the only cowboy I knew who wouldn't ride a horse. He could rope cattle and brand calves as well as most but simply refused to get up on a saddle. I never found out whether he had had a bad experience riding sometime or, like my mother, was just plain scared to get on one of the brutes. All he ever said by way of explanation was "If God had meant me to travel on four legs he would have given me four." He was a little baldheaded man, an A-number-one worker, and apparently chewed tobacco twenty-four hours a day. I was sure he chewed it in his sleep, and I figured he must have a special pocket in his cheek, like a gopher, where he stored it at mealtime. Anyway I never saw him without his cud. He bought either Star or Horseshoe brand plug tobacco in wholesale lots. Joe would pry the cover from the little wooden box that it came in, and I would get my nose nearly skinned because it was so close in order to get the first delicious fragrance from the closely packed bars.

For a long time I had pestered Joe for "just one little piece," but he and my father had refused to even discuss the idea with me. After dinner one noon I was especially persistent when Joe cut his after dinner "chaw." He started his usual automatic refusal, but my father stopped him. "You know, Joe," he said thoughtfully, "I think it's about time Mick started to chew tobacco."

At first Joe looked at my father in amazement, then finally catching on, nodded his head. "Guess you're right, Ed. If a man gets an early enough start, he can get to be a pretty good tobacco chewer in time."

He cut a small sliver from the plug and handed it to me. The first few bites were as sweet as I had expected. Then a very nasty taste, accompanied by a sort of paralysis, started in the back of my mouth, hurried into my throat, then raced on down to my stomach. I wiped the sweat and tears from my eyes and looked at my father. He looked awful—all blurry and tipped over to one side. I checked on Joe, but he was much worse. His mouth and nose and eyes had kind of run together, and he looked much smaller and farther away than he should. By now I knew that I had to get out of sight as fast as possible. The trip around the corner of the house and on behind our giant woodpile seemed endless, but I made it before I turned inside out.

Pretty soon my mother, who had disapprovingly watched the whole proceeding and had seen me disappear, came out the back door looking for me. She finally found me sprawled on the chips and sawdust.

"You all right?" she asked.

I nodded, not daring to try to talk.

She didn't say any more, just sat down on the freshly split stack of stovewood and hugged me up to her—a weak, white, and thoroughly cured tobacco chewer.

Big Jeff came to us along with our first herd of sheep. He drifted the twelve hundred Merinos down off the bench one afternoon in late August and headed them into the lane. I had gone along with my father to help funnel the sheep through and on over to the new shed, where they would be penned up for the night. As the last of the band approached the gate, a great grizzly bear of a man appeared out of the trailing dust, strolling along, handsignaling the two dogs that were flanking the nervous and loudly bleating sheep. When the last of the strays had dodged through the gate, the dogs nipping playfully at their heels, the herder strode up to my father and held out a huge hairy hand.

"Here's your woollies, M'sieu Chartrand," he roared giving our name its original French pronunciation. And he added as a sort of afterthought, "I'm Jeff."

His rolling *r*'s marked him as French and brought a pleased smile to my father's face. "*Bonjour,* Frenchman. *Comment ça va?*" he answered, wincing a little as his knuckles popped in the sheepherder's enthusiastic handshake.

"*Bon.*" Jeff rumbled. "Fine. Kind of dry and hungry, though. It was a long walk from Canada."

"Well, let's pen them up and go to the house for supper."

My first thought was that Jeff was made of hair. Great clouds of it, blue-black and curly, poured out from under the brim of his ragged ten-gallon hat. His rolled-up sleeves exposed huge fur-covered arms and hands, and his face was a wide wasteland of beard that reached almost to his belt buckle. But peering out through it were the brightest, bluest, friendliest eyes I had ever seen. And when he grinned at me, a wide band of square ivory teeth appeared. It was like the times Mrs. Quail opened the cover on her grand piano.

Jeff turned his cheerful gaze on me. "What's your name, boy?"

"Mick," I said.

Jeff let out a roar of laughter. "Hell, you don't look like no Irishman to me," he said, clapping me lightly on the back. That is, it was a light tap for him, but I went down as if I'd been kicked by a horse. I scrambled to my feet, gasping for breath and eyes smarting, but with a glow inside that promised me Jeff was going to be one of my best friends.

My father hired him before we reached the house, and he worked for us, off and on, for several years. From his great fund of experience he taught my father the practical side of sheep raising. He was a great favorite with my mother as well as with the rest of the family. But he did have one little fault. About once every six months he would draw his wages and go to town on a wild spree. When he got his normal senses back he would retrace his drinking route, apologizing to everyone and paying for the broken furniture and the contents of all the whisky bottles he had emptied. Then, dead broke again, he would make the long walk back to the ranch.

A brief, wildcat blizzard visited us one night in mid-August, leaving behind a foot of wet snow. It soon melted away under the hot summer sun, but our fields of ripened waist-high grain were now flattened into yellow carpets. At first, my father was in despair about the lost harvest. However, he was both stubborn and ingenious, and he devised some crude attachments for the binder that would enable him to save most of the crop. To make them required an overnight stay in Valier while Pete St. Denis forged and hammered out the required parts in his blacksmith shop.

My father readily agreed to my going along but hesitated a long minute when Jeff asked if he too could go. But he finally nodded assent. It had been several months since Jeff's last "vacation," and he had earned a couple days of fun.

"I'll make a deal with you," my father told Jeff, getting out his worn, snap-topped pocketbook and fishing out a twenty-dollar bill. "Here, take this to spend. I'll give you a check for the rest to take to the bank and start a savings account. You aren't so young anymore, Jeff. First thing you know you'll find yourself too old to work and not a dime to your name."

Jeff reared back as if he had run into a fourstrand barbed wire fence in the dark. The thought that he could get old had probably never entered his mind before. After a few minutes of digesting the new idea, he said, "By God, Ed. You're right. I'm going to quit blowing my money for whisky and save some while there's still time."

It was about noon the next day when we finished the ten mile drive and pulled up beside the blacksmith shop.

"Meet me here right after noon tomorrow, Jeff," my father said, and added, "and don't stop anywhere until you've banked your check."

Jeff was staring at the swinging doors of the saloon across the street. "Sure—sure, Ed. Gonna take care of it first thing."

But we both wondered if he was talking about his savings account or his thirst.

Shortly after lunch the next day, Louis St. Denis and I were having a grand time pretending to drive a huge traction engine that stood beside the blacksmith shop awaiting repairs when my father drove up from the livery stable and asked, "Where's Jeff?"

"We haven't seen him," we answered together.

"See if you can find him while I load up," he directed.

Finding him wasn't much of a job because Jeff was only a couple of blocks away and well advertised. A dozen or so men were standing around a telephone pole making insulting remarks to a lineman who was perched as near the top as he could possibly get. Jeff was sprawled on the ground, his back against the pole, his hat over his eyes—apparently asleep.

Some hours before (we learned from the bystanders) the lineman had stopped in the saloon for a quick one. Spotting Jeff slouched against the bar nearby, he made some unpleasant remarks about "Canucks" in general and crazy sheepherder ones in particular. Jeff hadn't bothered to answer, just walked over and lifted the man above his head, carried him to the door, and threw him into the street. When the badly shaken man had picked himself up, Jeff chased him up the nearest telephone pole, then sat down and went to sleep, to the great amusement of everyone.

By now the lineman was desperate. He was so tired he was afraid of falling off the pole, and he didn't dare come down and face Jeff.

"Someone take him away!" he pleaded.

This was received with loud laughs and catcalls. "Come on down, tough guy, and chase him away yourself," someone taunted.

But Jeff's intended victim just shook his head and muttered something about "not while that big ape's down there."

It was getting late so I pushed through the crowd and went over to the pole.

"Hey, Jeff," I said. "Come on! We gotta go home."

He pushed back his hat and looked at me with bleary eyes.

"I can't, Mick," he said. "Can't you see I'm busy?"

I looked around in amazement. "You ain't doing anything. Just sitting there," I argued. "Besides, you promised Pa you'd meet him at the blacksmith shop. He ain't going to like it if you don't."

Jeff thought that over carefully for a couple of minutes, then nodded. "All right. I made a promise, and I gotta keep it." He heaved himself to his feet. Then squinting up the pole, he raised a huge hairy fist and shook it threateningly. "Next time I come to town," he growled, "maybe there won't be a pole so handy."

"Next time you come to town, I won't even be in this damn *state!*" the lineman hollered as we walked away.

When we reached the wagon, my father eyed Jeff's torn and dusty clothes and his bleary eyes, but said nothing, just nodded toward the spring seat and clucked to the horses as soon as we were aboard.

Finally he said, staring off at the high blue mountains looming up ahead, "I hope you've got that bankbook safe somewhere."

Jeff looked blankly at him for a minute, then sadly shook his head, "Hell, Ed, I never got near any bank. You know and I know that I'll never be anything but a crazy sheepherder, with nothing to my name and broke two days after payday."

"Well you'll always have friends anyway, Jeff," my father consoled him. "Maybe in your case that's better than a bank account."

It was the cowboys though that put the spice into our ranch life. They were always on the lookout for fun and excitement, and no matter what happened, they never admitted to anything but the most casual expression of concern.

One time a family of gophers that I was trying to trap had set up housekeeping under the bank of a deep dried-up buffalo wallow near the lane. I went every day to inspect the steel trap I had set, hoping I had caught one of them and thereby proved to my father that I was smarter than they were—something I sometimes thought he doubted. So far the gophers were way ahead. One day I was glumly surveying the sprung and empty trap when the pounding hoofbeats of a galloping horse interrupted my dismal thoughts. It was my young cousin, Joe, more commonly known as "Tots," who had reached the age when he could do most of the things I wasn't even allowed to think about yet.

"Hey, Mick," he shouted as he raced toward the house. "How do you like my new horse?"

All thoughts of gophers and trapping vanished, and I lit out after him on a dead run. Tots had tied the little bay to a corral fence rail and was standing back admiring him when I panted through the gate.

"Got him for twenty bucks from a horse trader last night," he exulted. "Ain't he a beaut?"

I walked over for a closer look, being careful to stay on the horse's left as I had been taught.

"He don't look so big to me," I criticized. "Is he gentle?"

"Gentle as a kitten and smart as a whip," Tots boasted.

I stepped up and slapped him smartly on the rump as I had seen my father do so often to our gentle ranch horses. The next thing I knew I was sailing through the air backwards across the corral. I landed briefly on the seat of my pants, turned a couple reverse somersaults, and stopped face down in a deep layer of dirt and manure.

Tots, scared half out of his wits, picked me up and hurriedly examined me for cuts and bruises and broken bones. Aside from being completely winded and filthy dirty, I was in good shape. To cover up his badly shaken nerves, he walked over and picked up his fallen hat, slapped it against his leg to knock off the dust, then grinned at me. "Hell, Mick," he casually apologized, "I completely forgot to tell you he's an Indian horse." (Indian horses, as everyone knows, are handled strictly from the right.)

My cousins did not always emerge so scot-free from their lapses in memory and judgment. Late one August afternoon we were hauling in the last load of hay from the north meadow. I was driving, perched on the top of the beaverslide hayrack, while my father, Nolan (the hired man), and Frank were sprawled out behind me on the gently undulating hay. The team was giving me trouble because they would not pull together. Mike, one of our best workhorses, had been teamed up

with a recently acquired buckskin of doubtful character. All
day this big, rawboned goldbricker had been one step behind
his partner, a habit that was driving me and everyone else crazy.
Frank crawled up beside me and jabbed him in the backside
with the sharp tines of the pitchfork. Buck, as we called him,
just laid back his ears and switched his tail angrily but didn't
move any faster.

"Stubborn son-of-a-gun," Frank said, "or else dead on his
feet."

Nolan spoke up. "Bet he could be mean if he felt like it.
He's got a hammerhead and an ugly way of looking at you. Another thing, he's got a funny way of bunching up when you
throw a harness on him. He could be a real bucker."

"Bucker!" Frank laughed scornfully. "Why that old plug
couldn't dump old Mammy Johnson."

Old Mammy Johnson hadn't left her rocking chair without
help for the last ten years.

"I'm not so sure about Mammy," Nolan retorted sarcastically, "but I'll bet he can dump you."

Frank sat up and glared at Nolan, "I've got ten bucks that
says I can ride that glue-factory plug right into the ground."

"Okay! It's a bet" Nolan said. "Prove it."

"I'll just do that little thing," Frank snarled. "Right after
supper."

My mother let the dishes go that night, and we all went
down to the corral and sat in a long row on the top bar waiting
for the fun to start. Frank must have had some second thoughts
during supper about riding old Buck, for he proceeded rather
gingerly with the saddling operation.

The horse stood quietly enough though, just hunching a
little when Frank carefully put the blanket and then the saddle
on his back. But when he pulled the cinch up tight, Buck's ears
went back and his eyes rolled white, and he switched his tail vi-
ciously up and down several times.

My father called out, "Watch out, Frank. Looks like someone's tried to ride him before."

"Oh, he's just an old plug, I tell you." But it was plain that
Frank's confidence had slipped badly. He took the bandanna

from around his neck and, slipping the ends through the cheek-strap of the bridle, drew it across the horse's eyes, blindfolding him.

Old Buck stood dead still until Frank was settled in the saddle and had reached out and pulled the blindfold away. Then he crouched toward the ground and came up with a mighty leap, made a half turn in midair, and landed with all four legs stiff as fence posts. The rider by that time had lost his hat and taken on a dangerous list to the left. Without pause or hesitation, the fired-up nag repeated the maneuver, and as he landed, my cousin's long hair snapped across his eyes, temporarily blinding him. He had also lost one stirrup and the bridle reins and was unashamedly pulling leather with both hands. At the top of the third leap, Frank just kept on going straight up, took a long spread-eagled flight through the evening sky, and landed with a loud *whump* in the corral dust. Old Buck, without a backward glance, strolled up to the fence, neither showing a drop of sweat nor drawing an extra breath, and stood quietly waiting to be unsaddled.

Frank staggered up out of the dust he had raised and wobbled over to lean against the fence rails by my father's feet.

"Uncle Ed," he gasped. "Can you let me have ten dollars against next payday?"

Waking up on a summer morning, I would think of all the exciting things that might happen before I would have to call it a day and get back in bed. This day Frank and Leo were cutting and branding some calves they had driven into the corral the night before. Cutting—the common term used when referring to the castrating of young bull calves—was a rather unpleasant chore at best. My father never liked this part of cattle raising and, while it was going on, usually found he had something important to do elsewhere. Most of the time I was chased away at these times, but I did have a natural curiosity about the operation. There had been some talk about "rocky mountain oysters" the night before down at the bunkhouse, and I was especially anxious to be on hand that day to find out just what my smart-alec cousins were talking about.

It always seemed to me that when I had something special

on my mind, the chores piled up like crazy. That morning turned out to be one of the worst of the summer. First I had to dry the dishes while Iris washed at a maddeningly slow pace. Then my mother ordered me to fill up the empty woodbox, and in my hurry to get it done, I left the back door open, allowing a million or so flies to take over the kitchen. When she finally stopped taking my head off, we all got dishtowels and flailed away, driving the flies out again. Then just as I reached the door, Iris informed my mother that the waterpail was empty. Examination proved that there was still a good cupful of water in the bucket and that Iris was a dirty liar. We were just squaring off when my mother grabbed me by the hair with one hand and the waterpail with the other and started us both on our way to the spring house. So the branding was well along when I crawled through the corral bars and approached the small fire used for heating the branding irons. Several calves stood by the fence, as far away as possible from my cousins, shivering and bawling. Frank and Leo were hunkered down by the fire, one turning a branding iron so that it would heat evenly, the other one roasting something on a willow twig. I eyed the small gob of meat and then the wailing calves.

"What's that you're cooking?" I asked suspiciously.

"Why that's a rocky mountain oyster," Leo said. "We're saving it for you."

By now I was sure where it had come from, and I backed off a couple of steps.

"We eat them. All cowboys eat them," Frank said; and he held the stick out to me.

I backed away another step and shoved my hands deep into my pockets. "I ain't hungry," I said hastily, and I wasn't lying. The very thought of not acting like a real cowboy in front of my two heroes was impossible, but it was equally impossible for me to dine on the tender parts of those poor grieving calves over by the fence.

Luckily for me, my father chose this moment to drop by to see how things were going. He took in the situation at a glance and suggested that I beat it back to the house. I never learned what he said to my two shamefaced cousins, but they never again invited me to share a rocky mountain oyster barbecue with them.

But my cousins, and Johnny Pfeiffer, and Cliff Miller, and some of the other young cowboys were much more than just friends to me. They represented everything a half-grown boy could possibly want to be. I blindly ignored all the humdrum work they had to do, plowing and planting in the spring, putting up the hay crop in the summer, following the threshing machine every fall, digging postholes in the dry flinty soil, and stringing unmeasured miles of barbed wire. There was something about the tilt of their Stetson hats, the angle at which a freshly rolled Bull Durham cigarette dangled from a lip, the sound of the running jingle of their spurs as they strode across the porch floor, the casual way they stepped into a saddle, that spelled glamour to me. I was determined to pattern my life after theirs and some day become one of their vanishing tribe.

The Runaway

THE SUMMER I WAS EIGHT YEARS OLD, Iris and I had a big fight, and I decided to run away from home. My parents had gone to Aunt Minnie's to see the new baby, and I was some miles downstream by the time my mother came rattling across the prairie with her horse and buggy, and caught up with me. She was scared and mad, and the licking she gave me with the horsewhip discouraged me from trying that again in a hurry. And what happened to George Fisher a year later when he ran away cured me of running away for the rest of my life.

Among our nearer neighbors were the Fishers, who lived several miles downstream from us and who owned one of the larger ranches around. Their house was finished off with clapboards and painted white, something unusual in a time of log houses and dirt roofs. Montana was a lonely country, and it was a comfort to know you had neighbors. But a ranch was a busy place, and none of us had much time for visiting back and forth except during slack times. We saw each other mostly when there was a box-social and dance at the schoolhouse or a Fourth of July picnic, or when we would lend a hand at each other's threshings or barn raisings.

George Fisher was almost twice my age and an only child. It seemed to me that he had about everything a boy could ask for, but he wasn't spoiled or wild and could do a good day's work on the ranch. Like most boys he learned to ride almost as soon as he walked. Before he was ten, he had his own horse and saddle, and by the time he was twelve, he was an expert rider. When he reached fifteen, he seemed a full-grown man to me. He loved to hunt and had already made a trip into the high mountains to the west with some older men. These mountains that formed the Continental Divide were wild and rugged, an ideal home for Rocky Mountain goats, grizzly bears, mountain lions, deer, and timber wolves. Except for a few cabins where some of the old-time hunters and trappers spent their winters, no one lived there. The game trails that led over the passes were hard to follow even in summer and were virtually impassable in winter. Men sometimes hunted along the logging trails on the lower slopes but seldom ventured above timberline.

Mark Fisher, George's father, was a hard, rough-talking man but was fair to his help and paid well. His wife, Anna, was the opposite, a quiet, even-tempered woman of Norwegian descent. There wasn't a better cook in all Teton County, or a better housekeeper. She even managed to keep the small plot of grass in front of their house alive and green through the long, dry summer, and the silvery cottonwood trees she had planted grew tall and strong through the bitter cold of the winters. The ranch hands ate with the Fishers in their long, low-ceilinged kitchen with its wonderful smells. I used to like nothing better than to stay and have a meal with them.

That was the year my father decided to go in for sheep raising, which meant building a large sheep shed and yards. One afternoon my father and I hitched a four-horse team to the running gear of the heavy Studebaker wagon and set out for the Fisher place to bring back a load of lumber that we were buying. While the men were loading the wagon, a horse trader with a small string of saddle-broken cow ponies pulled in and was invited to spend the night. By the time the last plank was aboard and the binder tightened, it was time to eat, and we, too, were expected to stay for supper. We all trooped up to the house for a tremendous meal of steak, potatoes, fresh-baked bread, and canned peach shortcake. Then all of us except Mrs. Fisher went down to the corral to look the horses over and maybe do some horse trading.

Everyone spotted him at once—a beautiful coal-black gelding. George, I could see, wanted that horse. His father and the trader saw it, too. "He's all he looks to be, Mr. Fisher," the trader said, "well broken and gentle. The boy couldn't find a better horse in the state of Montana."

Under the watchful eye of his father, George caught and saddled the horse. Then, swinging astride, they drummed off down the lane at a rocking-horse gallop. A few minutes later they were back, and George dismounted in front of his father and looked up into his stern face. Without saying anything, Mr. Fisher turned to the horse, ran knowing hands over him, and then, standing back, looked him over searchingly. Finally, he turned to the trader and nodded his approval. George, speechless with thanks, grasped the black mane and grinned. He turned to me and said, "I'm going to call him Satan, Mick. How's that?"

In a moment they were all talking at once. Horse talk. I was a pretty avid pint-sized horseman myself and had been busy getting a better look at Satan. His satiny coat fascinated me. I *had* to touch it! I reached out and stroked him near the flank. Like released springs, his two hind feet flew out in a savage kick. The men ducked and swore, but George and I were too scared to move. George gripped the reins, holding the cringing, dancing horse. My father, his face stone white, grabbed me. When he saw I was all right, he gave me a shake that jerked my pants loose. "What the hell's the matter with you?" he yelled. "You know better than to do a thing like that!" My father almost never raised a hand to us kids, or his voice either, so I knew he'd had a real scare.

Mr. Fisher was roaring, "That black bastard! Get him off the place. I won't have him around. He could kick somebody's brains out."

"It wasn't his fault," George pleaded. "Mick scared him. Lots of horses kick when they're scared."

"That's right," the trader quickly agreed. "You know how horses are."

"No. No deal," Mr. Fisher insisted. "I won't have a kicking horse on the ranch."

My father's reputation as a horse breeder and trainer was well known throughout the area, and his opinions about horses carried considerable weight. "He don't look mean to me," he said. Turning to the trader, he asked, "Where'd you get him?"

"Bob Williams. Over near Cutbank. You must know him. He claimed the horse was gentle."

"He spooks easy, most likely," my father concluded. "Might never happen again. But you've got to be careful around him."

Mr. Fisher hesitated a long time. "Well," he said slowly, "if we do keep him, he's never to be put into the barn so anybody'd have to walk behind him. You understand, George?"

George grinned and leaped into the saddle and took off. We all stood by the fence and watched him go.

By the middle of June our new sheep shed was framed and ready to be shingled. This called for a shingling bee. Some of the ranchers would come with their families and hired hands for the day. The men, working almost shoulder to shoulder, could easily finish the roof by chore time.

Early Saturday morning I was swinging on the polegate that opened into the wagon yard, anxiously watching for the first arrivals, when I heard the distant drumming of hooves. It seemed only a second later that George, on Satan, came round the corner of the lane, tore across the long flat with mane, tail, and jacket flying in the wind, and swung through the open gate to a sliding stop in the middle of the yard. Chickens scattered with loud squawks and drifting feathers, and Monday, our usually quiet Newfoundland sheepdog, raced around barking like mad. The rest of the arrivals were far less spectacular.

After the noon dinner the men rested for a while in the shade of the porch. The talk soon turned to the coming Fourth of July picnic and its big climax, the horse race. My cousin Frank, a veteran horseman of eighteen, called over to George in a loud, challenging voice. "That Satan's not a bad-looking cayuse. You going to race him?"

George's answer was short and quick. "He's the best horse in the county. Of course I'm going to race him!"

"I'm riding Uncle Ed's Snort" Frank drawled "and I've got ten bucks that says Satan can't beat him!"

Mark Fisher spoke up. "Okay, George. Race your horse if you want to. But no betting. When you grow up will be time enough for that."

Now I was in trouble. Snort, my father's big bay quarter horse, had been my idol for a long time, and was conceded to be the finest cow pony for miles around. I'd seen him win that Fourth of July race for two straight years. But lately I'd grown almost as proud of Satan. Now which one would I pull for?

On the morning of the Fourth, I was so excited I didn't even quarrel with my sister about helping with the dishes. All I could think about was the race. I was the first of us five kids to be scrubbed and dressed and dismissed with my mother's automatic, "Now sit down somewhere and keep clean." Only I couldn't sit still and had soon edged my way out to help the men get things ready. The two-seater Democrat wagon had already been pushed into the creek and scrubbed 'til its black body and yellow wheels sparkled in the sunlight. The horses were curried until every bay hair gleamed beneath the freshly oiled harness. Now some axle grease for the wheels and we would be off. Only, in helping, I somehow managed to smear more grease on myself than on the axles, delaying the departure while I was dragged to the house by an irate mother to change into my second-best shirt and an old pair of patched and faded pants. By the time we finally reached the picnic grounds, nearly everyone else was there. The tables were set up under the cottonwoods beside Fish Lake, the teams tied to the pole fence, and the racecourse, which was only a quarter mile of newly cut meadow, stretched invitingly beyond.

While the men listened to some long-winded political speeches, the women made coffee on the hastily built fireplaces and unpacked bowls of salad, jars of pickles, pans of baked beans, layer cakes, and mason jars of lemon juice for the lemonade. We kids milled around and tormented everybody to hurry up with the eats. When we finally sat down, I ate so much and so fast that I soon found myself refusing such heavenly things as coconut layer cake and chocolate walnut fudge. I wasn't exactly sick, but it was a while before I got back into the swing of things again.

Even when my stomach began to feel better, the three-legged races, the gunnysack race, the tug-of-war, catching the greased pig, and the climb up the greased pole to capture the five-dollar bill didn't seem to be as exciting as usual. I couldn't wait for four o'clock to come, the time set for the horse race.

At last it did. About a dozen horses and riders gathered at the starting line. Almost at once, after the starter's pistol shot, the two favorites were running neck and neck, ahead of the rest. I heard myself yelling, "Come on Satan! Come on Snort!" I hopped up and down about ready to explode with excitement, cheering on the two straining animals, their manes and tails streaming in the wind, George and Frank leaning far over the saddle horns. Then a mighty roar went up from the spectators and the race was over—Satan the winner by an eyelash. After the crowd thinned out, I went up to George. "Old Snort gave you a run for your money, anyway," I said. "But Satan sure can run!"

George grinned at me. "Want a ride on him?"

"Me?"

"Sure. He rides double. Jump on back, and I'll take you for a turn. Hang on now."

I felt the smooth motion of Satan beneath me as George let him out. He went like the wind, and I held on tight. When he stopped, I felt almost as if I had won the race myself.

We finished haying late that year. It was almost September by the time we were drawing in the last load. My father and

Frank were sprawled on the hay in back. I was perched up in front, driving Mike and Jim, our matched pair of heavy Belgian bays, toward the large haystack near the feeding corral where the stack would be topped off and weighted down against the fall winds. As we turned the corner of the barn, I saw the Fishers' hired man, Bill Tokin, riding across the pasture toward the house. He didn't come up our way very often and therefore I figured he had some news to tell.

"Bill Tokin's coming across the field," I called out.

The men sat up and watched the horse and rider approach. "Wonder what's up?" Frank said. We met him at the haystack.

"You folks heard about Satan? George's got to sell him."

"Sell him? Satan? Why? What's happened?" The questions tumbled out of my mouth.

"He kicked the missus. George put him in the wrong stall in the barn. Forgot his father's warning, I guess. You know how kids are." He hurried on, "Oh, she's all right. But it could have been real bad. She was looking for eggs in the mangers and came in sudden-like. Good thing she was close, got more pushed than kicked. Mark says George can't keep Satan now. You know how he is. The boy disobeyed, he's got to be punished."

"Maybe he'll change his mind," Frank ventured, but my father shook his head. "I doubt it. That's not Mark Fisher's way."

And he didn't. Satan was sold, and I guess there was a big row because, as Bill reported later, George and his father weren't speaking to each other. Mrs. Fisher tried to take the boy's part, and that made things worse. Bill said he didn't think he'd stay on much longer. "Mr. Fisher used to be a pretty good man to work for," he said, "but not any more. He's got so he's ornery with everybody. Him and the boy never did hit it off too good. But George won't take so much any more. He's pretty stubborn too, you know. He'll run off some of these days. You'll see."

I didn't see much of George after Satan was sold, but I heard considerable talk among the grownups. One day our neighbors, the Howes, had come to spend the day and Mrs. Howe and my mother were rocking on the porch. I had sneaked in the back door to steal some cookies when I heard George's name mentioned.

Mrs. Howe said, "The ranch hands say he beats the boy and won't let him off the place. George is turning pretty sullen, too, and you can't blame him for—"

"Somebody ought to do something," my mother broke in angrily.

"It wouldn't do any good. Mark's got his mind made up to break the boy just like he'd break a bronc, and nobody's going to stop him."

Another time my father had been to the Fisher ranch, and I heard him talking to my mother afterwards. "I told the damn fool not to be so hard on the boy."

"What did he say?" my mother asked.

"Just said George had to learn who was boss on that ranch. Said he'd given in once against his better judgment and look what had happened! And besides he wasn't going to be told by a fifteen-year-old boy when he could sell a horse and when he couldn't."

So when we heard that George had run off and was hiding in the Blackfoot Indian reservation, we weren't surprised. I guess it was a couple of weeks later that my father and I drove into town. We'd just got out of the wagon in front of Sam Harris's store and were stretching our legs when we saw a mud-spattered buckboard with two passengers in it. It clattered across the bridge and came up the street. Mark sat straight in the seat, his face grim as he barely nodded in answer to the greetings of the townspeople. George slumped in the seat with downcast eyes, completely ignoring us all as they rolled by and headed toward home.

"He's got him," I said in disgust.

"Yeah," Sam said. "The Indian Agent sent word day before yesterday that they had George over at Browning. Didn't take Mark long to get the boy back, did it?"

"Will they put George in jail now for running away?" I asked.

"No, no," Mr. Harris said. "The law just gets word to somebody to come fetch him if a boy runs off. They have to do that.

George is still under age, you know."

"Quit worrying about him, Mick," my father said. "He'll be all right." But he didn't sound too sure of it himself, and I couldn't stop seeing George's half-hidden face and how sad it looked.

The biggest event of the fall on the ranch was threshing the oat and wheat harvest. When threshing day came, I was stuck with my usual job of carrying water, and the gallons of it that that thirsty crew could drink and spill in the course of a day would put a herd of elephants to shame. George, quiet and sad, drove one of the rigs that shuttled back and forth between the grainfield and the machine. He only stopped once for a drink, and since there wasn't anybody close by, I screwed up my courage and asked in a loud whisper, "You going to run away again?" He looked startled, but then his face grew grim and his lower lip stuck way out. "You can just bet I am," he hissed. "Next time I'm going so far he'll never find me!"

Winter set in early that year. The wind roared in from Canada, driving the snow into deep drifts in the gullies and on the hillsides. Each day the temperature dropped a little lower. My father said he couldn't recall a colder December in the twenty years he'd lived in Montana.

"We won't be able to get into town to pick up the Christmas order from Sears-Roebuck if it doesn't let up," my mother worried.

It was Saturday afternoon. Bitterly cold. Frank, my father, and I were down in the bunkhouse. A sudden storm had blown in from the north an hour earlier, whipping the fine snow so hard against the windows that it sounded like hail. The grindstone was set up in the middle of the room, and I turned it while Frank sharpened a double-bitted ax. My father was filing a six-foot crosscut saw clamped in a vise by the window. It was warm and cosy with the black sheet-iron stove glowing red and the cold busily painting frost pictures on the window panes. Suddenly, the door was thrown open and Mark Fisher, followed by Bill Tokin, stomped in.

"Have you seen George?" Mark burst out. There was a

scared look in his eyes that I had never expected to see.

My father and Frank exchanged glances. "No," they said together. "What's happened?"

"He's took off again. Bill here says he saw him start out three, four hours ago on horseback headed this way. I don't know why the hell he didn't tell me sooner."

"It wasn't so cold then, and anyway I figured—"

Mr. Fisher interrupted him. "I think he's headed over the mountains for Chick Grimsley's hunting camp. He's been there before. Knows Chick's up there. They'll take care of him if he can make it."

"He hasn't got a chance! Not in *this* weather," my father answered, tossing the file onto the workbench. "Frank, get some warm clothes on and saddle the horses. Mick, run and tell your mother that we're going after George. You men get thawed out. Stoke up the fire. We'll be ready in a few minutes."

Ten minutes later the four men headed west toward the jagged peaks that towered in the afternoon sky. The logging roads and game trails would be drifted too deep in most places for the horses to do anything but flounder. In my mind's eye I could see George leading his horse by the reins, tramping along, his heavy boots leaving dark holes in the clean white snow, his face set, his breath steaming, his heart set on just one thing—to get away from his father. I felt sick thinking about him out there, and I couldn't keep away from the windows. By dark it had cleared some, and the moon shone out every once in a while between passing clouds, making it look colder yet. Finally, during one of these clear spells, I spied them coming down the hillside toward the house, like a file of ghosts, their hoofbeats muffled in the snow.

"Here they come!" I hollered.

"Where?" my mother was at the window, pushing me to one side. But the moon had gone behind a cloud. "Have they got him? I can't make out."

"There's just the four of them," I said, my eyes straining to see the men and beasts, clad in sinister grey hoar frost and dusted over with powdered snow. My mother turned away, and

I heard her go the the stove and jam in more wood and slam the lids, rattling pots and pans, getting dinner for the famished, half-frozen men.

"Sorry, Mick," Frank said when he came in and saw my face. "but we lost his trail up there on a bare ridge. No point in going on then. But he'll be all right. We'll go back first thing in the morning."

"He's got food and blankets," Mr. Fisher said. His face didn't look mad anymore, just tired and old. "He's no greenhorn. We've hunted up there. I always made him do his share of camp work. He knows how to take care of himself."

"He'll find a fir thicket," my father chimed in, "and build a lean-to, light a good fire—there's plenty of blowdown wood— and keep it going all night. Tomorrow we'll likely meet him coming back." But his voice didn't sound as cheerful as his words.

The men ate, planning on how to get snowshoes and fresh horses for the morning. They'd start at daybreak, they said.

When Mr. Fisher and Bill had left, my mother turned to my father. "Mark Fisher's changed his tune," she said. "What happened?"

"He didn't say much. Said George must have been planning another try first chance he got. He had food and blankets stashed away in the barn, and an ax and a rifle. It's plain now that Mark wishes he'd listened to his wife and the rest of us."

I went back to the window, scratched a new hole in the frost, and stood looking out. The moon was bright now, reflecting on the gleaming snow crystals, and there was a steady snapping and crackling as the frost bit deep into the log walls and pulled loose the nails in the porch floor. I shivered, thinking of George crouching over a small fire high up on some desolate ridge of those cruel white mountains. I knew it was one of the coldest nights we had ever had.

I got up at daybreak next morning, but the men had already gone from the kitchen. It was a terrible day of waiting. The thermometer read forty-five degrees below zero. My mother and the schoolteacher cried and drank tea and even worked

some. Part of the time they tried to be cheerful and talk with us
kids, but I didn't feel like talking and spent most of the day on
the half-empty woodbox beside the stove, listening for the
sound of voices outside telling of the men's return.

With typical Montana fickleness the weather changed, and
by noon it was up to zero. We began to feel more hopeful. My
peephole in the frosted pane grew as the sun hit it, and I didn't
have to put my face so close to see out anymore.

Just about sunset the horse-drawn bobsled came in sight
with the line of searchers following single file on horseback.
"They're coming!" I called out. Then as they drew nearer, my
heart began to pound. I could hardly breathe. That stiff slab-
like thing under the blanket on the bob—that was George's frozen body! At our gate my father and Frank turned off and went
into the barn to put up their horses, the rest of the procession
continuing on down the lane and out of sight.

My mother too had seen. She moved slowly over to the
stove and set the coffeepot on to boil. I heard the men come
stomping throught the door and watched as they pulled off lay-
ers of heavy clothing. No one spoke.

When the men sat down to heaping plates of ham and eggs
and cups of scalding coffee, their words started falling out. The
others gathered round to listen, but I slipped silently back to
my seat on the woodbox beside the stove.

George, they said, must have gotten well into the mountains by dark. On the open prairie the wind had swept the snow
thin, and the horse could travel easy and fast. But he must have
abandoned the pony when he came to the deep snow of the forest and struck off on foot for the Grimsley camp. When it got
too dark to travel, he had done as my father had predicted.
There, among the thick young firs they found his bedroll, a
lean-to of fresh-cut boughs over it and, in front, a small, carefully laid campfire of dry shavings and twigs with heavier
wood nearby. A scorched spot among the shavings showed the
boy's desperate try to start a fire with his only match. In his
agony of fear and despair when he realized he had run off in
such rage and hurry that he had forgotten matches, he appar-

ently had started to run wildly down the hill. And stepping on a sheet of snow-covered ice, he must have slid down a steep bank and become helplessly wedged beneath a huge fallen pine tree. They found him there under the bright noon sun, his face like polished marble, his gun still clutched in his frozen fingers.

Christmas and the Comet

ONE NIGHT WHEN I was eight years old, my father, who had stepped outdoors before going to bed to take a weather-wise look at the sky, stuck his head back through the half-open kitchen door and called to me, "Come on out, Mick; I want to show you something." I followed him out and around the woodpile to where we could get a good view to the west. The clear, moonless night was brightly lit by a large star blazing high in the sky, trailed by a curved and narrowing band of silver that reached down almost to the mountaintops. It was the most beautiful thing I had ever seen, and I stared at it in wonder.

"That's Halley's Comet," he said. "And that long streak hanging down is its tail. Nobody knows much about it except that it disappears and comes back again every seventy-five years."

I was both fascinated and frightened by its unearthly appearance. Later my mother and Frank joined us and we stood gazing at it for a long time.

One afternoon later in the summer, my younger sister Lucy and my cousin Ninnie and I were wading in the icy water that came down from the high snowfields and flowed past our house, when I cut my little toe on a sharp stone. It seemed a pretty good cut to me, so I took off for the house spouting blood and tears in about equal amounts. My mother stopped me at the kitchen door and took in the situation at a glance. Operating on her rule-of-thumb that kids who cried loud were seldom hurt much, she told me to sit down on the porch and wait. "I've just mopped the kitchen floor and don't want blood all over it."

After a quick inspection she said it wasn't much of a cut and got a pan of warm soapy water and part of an old bedsheet to tear into a bandage. She had just finished tying up the clean white cloth (which didn't match the dirty old one on my big toe—the result of poor aim with the ax while chopping kindling a couple of days before) when she looked down the lane and saw Lily coming. Lily was my young married cousin, who lived four miles upstream from us and who already had several children—all girls. They had gone by on their way to Dupuyer in the morning and were now stopping again on their way home.

After she tied the team to a fencepost in the lane, the girls scrambled out and joined Lucy and Ninnie at the creek. Lily, meanwhile, hauled our grainbag of groceries from the back of the buckboard, recovered the small handful of mail from under the seat cushion, and walked up the path to the house, stopping beside me where I was sitting with my bloodstained bandage in good view, hoping for some words of sympathy.

"What happened to you?" she wanted to know.

"Nothing but a scratch on his toe" my mother said—heartlessly, I thought. "What's the news?"

Lily carefully scrutinized the letters before handing them over. "A letter from your sister Annie in Helena. Uncle Ed's got a bill or something from the J. I. Case Company, and here's your paper—the *Acantha*. That's all I guess."

My mother tore open the letter from Aunt Annie and skimmed through it quickly.

"Everything's fine with her, and she's coming for a few day's visit. Louis can't leave the store, so she's coming alone."

"She's lucky," Lily said. "No kids to think about—can do anything she likes."

My mother snorted disdainfully, "Well, I'll take my kids!

She's welcome to her lonesome fun."

She laid the letter to one side and picked up the paper. Lily walked to the edge of the porch and called down to the kids still wading in the creek, "Come on up, all of you. I've got a peppermint stick for everyone."

There was a mad scramble as they ran screaming and pushing onto the porch. She had just passed out the last of the red and white striped candy when my mother gave a slow whistle.

"Remember that comet we all saw not so long ago? Well, listen to this," and she read from the paper: " 'Scientists think that if the world should pass through the tail of it, the poisonous gas it contains might kill all living things on our planet. It would be the end of the world.' "

We all looked at her in stricken silence. Finally Ninnie's chin began to tremble, and she came out with a loud wail, "We're all going to die."

It was a terrible moment and all at once my cut toe didn't seem like much.

"Does it really say that?" Lily demanded, reaching for the paper.

But my mother pushed her away and continued—reading to herself now. Finally, she looked up with a sigh of relief and said, "They say there's only one chance in a million that it could happen and not to worry about it. The damn fools to scare us like that!"

Ninnie was finally convinced that she wasn't going to die right away and stopped crying. Lucy just tossed her head—"I wasn't scared anyway," she said—and they all went back to playing in the creek.

But I sat on the porch and thought about that million-in-one chance and wondered if this might not be that particular time. I wondered how we would die. Would we kick and jerk like dogs or coyotes did when they ate meat poisoned with strychnine? Or would we just go to sleep and never wake up again? I looked at my mother and at Lily, and they didn't seem worried. But I just couldn't forget, the way the paper said to.

The following Wednesday my father and I went to Dupuyer to meet my mother's sister and bring her home for a week's visit. We were standing in front of Harris Brothers' store, along with a number of the townspeople who were waiting around for the stage, when the high-wheeled, stiff-sprung wagon rolled up the dusty street and stopped in front of us. A floater cowboy sat in front with the driver; Aunt Annie, looking tired and mad, sat behind them; and a drummer with his sample case beside him occupied the last seat. My aunt's normally florid face had turned a light purple from the heat of the afternoon sun, and her heavy mass of bright red hair, which she wore piled high on her head, had slipped a little because of the jolting of the wagon. As a result, the wide-brimmed straw hat that was pinned to it with a couple of gold-headed hatpins was now at a rakish angle over one ear. She looked down at my father and me with a pair of flashing blue eyes and smiled grimly.

"Hello, Annie," my father said. "Have a good trip?"

"A good trip!" She had a kind of hoarse, grating voice that carried well. "My God, Ed. After riding forty miles in this—" She stopped and looked around at the grinning faces below her, "—this *blasted* thing, I'm just about dead!"

Aunt Annie always spoke her mind strongly and to the point, and her speech always sounded funny to me. We were used to my mother's light, cheerful cockney tones, but her sister's voice was slower and heavier with a very broad accent. "Yorkshire," my mother said it was, because she had lived many years with relatives in that part of England.

My father helped her down and pulled a huge wicker suitcase from under the seat, along with a large parcel wrapped in brown paper and tied with a heavy cord. She stood firmly planted in the middle of the wooden sidewalk and glanced up and down the street. She took in the store, the Dell Hotel, a couple of nondescript buildings that housed the offices of the town clerk and our one lawyer, and a saloon. Across the street was another saloon and farther down the weatherbeaten livery stable.

She shook her head despairingly and glared, first at me and then at my father.

"Look at this dump! And look at you two! You look like a couple of tramps."

I had started from home with perfectly clean (though well-patched and faded) shirt and overalls but had spent the best part of an hour with Louis St. Denis in his father's black-smith shop and had managed to pick up a good coating of soot and wagon grease and just plain barn filth. My long shaggy hair hadn't been cut in months, and I was tanned dark as an Indian. My father too could have stood a haircut and even a shave. He had on clean clothes, but his pants hadn't been pressed in years, and the vest he always wore to town was wrinkled and lacking a couple of buttons. But his beautiful light-tan cattleman's hat was set jauntily on his head with just the hint of a tilt over his right eye.

I looked blankly at my unfamiliar aunt, wondering what on earth was the matter with her. My father was the strongest and smartest and handsomest man in Teton County. Anybody would have to be blind not to see that. And my father too looked rather amazed. He saw me looking so much worse most of the time that he considered me quite presentable just now. Neither of us said anything. After all, what could you say to a woman who talked like that?

She pointed a stubby forefinger practically in my father's face and continued loud enough for all the town to hear, "How can you bury your children and Emma in this awful hole?" She and my grandfather were the only two people I knew who used my mother's given name. Everyone else called her Peggy, so I had to think twice before I was sure whom she meant.

Several of the men standing around snickered and winked at my father, but he just grinned in his easy way and said quietly, "Hell, Annie. This is the finest town in the state."

"Ed," she said, "I believe you really mean that. And you're lucky you feel that way," Her face suddenly relaxed into a wide and friendly smile, and miraculously she was our kindly, loving aunt, who always remembered our birthdays with a card and a gift, and sent a huge wooden box filled with the most wonderful presents every Christmas.

My father picked up the suitcase while I wrestled with the package, and we started for the wagon standing by the store hitching rail.

Aunt Annie stayed a week and spent most of her time fishing. She had been a successful angler for many years but only as a "worm dunker." Recently bitten by the dry-fly bug, she insisted on practicing this art almost every day. Sheep Creek, though small, was fed by the melting snows of the Continental Divide and always ran a good stream of clear trout water even during the heat of summer. Being an ardent fisherman didn't prevent her from also remaining a modest lady, however, and she appeared in the morning dressed in a high-necked, long-sleeved dress, the skirt of which was tucked into a voluminous pair of bloomers. They had been cut out with a lavish hand and drooped from her waist like sails on a becalmed schooner.

After breakfast she would pull on a pair of lady's gum boots and an old ten-gallon hat of Frank's, her long red hair braided and wound around her head so that the hat would fit.

"Come on, Mick," she would say. "Let's go get a basketful." And with a nod from my mother we would start out.

When we reached the first big pool above the house, she would stop and pull her flybook from a secret pocket in those flapping bloomers, cast her eye around, then hold up a wet forefinger. "Let's see," she would say to our fresh Montana morning, "west wind and clear sky. Guess I'd better use a royal coachman."

No matter what the wind or weather was that day or any other day, she always decided on a coachman. It was probably the only fly she knew for sure, and it was, no doubt, as good as any as far as she was concerned.

She looped the fly on the six-foot gut leader and, after a few false casts, shot it out into the stream. Her forecast was pretty good, but she never paid the slighest attention to the back-cast. As a result, I didn't do much fishing myself but spent most of the day climbing around in the cottonwoods and willows, retrieving her lure.

One day I asked her about the nagging worry in the back of my mind. "Aunt Annie," I said, "do you think we're going to get killed by the comet?"

She stopped her false casting and stared at me as if I had suddenly lost my mind. "What are you talking about, boy?"

I backed off a couple of steps, then screwed up my courage to go on. "Mama read in the paper that we might all get poisoned by the comet's tail."

"Oh. *That* comet," she answered briskly. "Well, I don't think those old white-whiskered goats know which way is up, let alone what a comet's tail is made of when it's a million miles away. Besides, there's nothing we or anyone else can do about it anyway, so why worry? Come on, let's fish!" and she reeled in her line ready to move on to the next pool, a hundred feet upstream and guarded by a tight ring of hook-snatching cottonwoods.

One afternoon we returned home with an especially fine catch of brook trout, and Aunt Annie bragged to my father that it was probably the finest catch of fish ever taken from the stream. He just smiled in a superior way and said, "Shucks, Annie, twenty-five fish are nothing. I went out one morning last June and was back in a hour with over a hundred, some over sixteen inches long."

Aunt Annie's quick temper flared up. "You're just like all fishermen, Ed Shatraw," she declared. "A damn liar. And if you think you can get me mad, you can just think again!" And she stamped off to her room to change from her fishing gear.

Later he confessed to her that the fish he had caught had swum from the main stream down the big irrigation ditch and out through the diversion channels to become stranded in the thick meadow grass. He had simply walked around picking them up until he had a filled gunnybag.

Another thing Aunt Annie took very seriously was her religion. She was a dedicated Episcopalian and a pillar of St. Peter's Church in Helena. She looked upon Old Man Moon and his Free Methodist ideas as nothing short of criminal.

"Don't let that old man convert the children from the true faith," she warned my mother one day. "What *will* become of them out in this uncivilized place, anyway? No church or Sunday school! Why, they're little better than heathens as it is."

My mother rushed to our defense. "Old Moon is a good man and thinks the world of the kids. He's never hurt them. Besides, we go to church every time they hold services at the schoolhouse. Last year we went three times." She might have added that we went mostly because we liked the hymn singing and the visiting with the neighbors afterward. The religious aspect of the services was largely wasted on us.

Usually when Aunt Annie visited us, we talked about Christmas presents, too. One evening I got out the catalog and pointed out to her the one thing I wanted most in the world. It was a motion-picture machine "that throws real moving pictures on a white sheet," so the description read. I had never seen a motion picture and couldn't figure out how it could possibly work, but I didn't question it because they called it a "Magic Lantern."

I knew from past experience that Santa paid considerable attention to my aunt's suggestions. But it cost almost five dollars, such an enormous sum that I was pretty sure it was out of the question.

Aunt Annie read the item about it very carefully and kind of shook her head.

"Sure costs a lot," I said sadly. "Don't it, Aunt Annie?"

She looked at me with her sharp blue eyes that seemed to see right into my head. "Maybe Santa can do something about it," she rumbled in her baritone whisper, and I cheered up some.

The days hurried by and all at once it was time for our aunt to pack her bag and her fishing gear and go back to that vague place where she lived with Uncle Louis. We had enjoyed her visit and missed her lively company, but there was an air of relaxation around the supper table the first evening after she left that had been missing the past week.

"Feels kind'a good to be just our own ornery selves again," Frank remarked comfortably. And he was right. Company seemed somehow to cramp our style.

A few weeks later the new teacher arrived and soon settled into our lives as a member of the family.

As usual, I fell violently in love with her. Grace was so pretty and stylish and so nice to us kids that at first I couldn't believe she was real. In a very short time, though, she began to seem more human. She started to expect a lot from me, like bringing in wood for the school chunk stove, keeping the water-pail filled, beating the chalk dust out of erasers, studying the times table, and knowing the meaning of a lot of outlandish words such as "refractory." It was over this word that I began to see Grace in her true light.

In our school there were seven kids so distributed in age that we had seven grades. I was the only one in my class for five years, so when recitation time came, there was no hope that chance would come to my rescue and someone else would answer the questions I didn't know. I was reading aloud *The King of the Golden River,* a chapter a day, and was having rough going of it. I finally reached the part where the dwarf visits Gluck during a heavy rainstorm, and in describing the dwarf, the author said his cheeks were as red as if he were trying to blow out a "refractory" fire. Naturally, Grace asked me if I knew what the word meant. After some wild guessing, in which time I got the whole school in an uproar, she accused me of being a smart-alec and ordered me to go stand in the corner.

I went, feeling hurt and mad, and stared resentfully at the rough log wall. Almost immediately, though, I discovered a small colony of carpenter ants busily working on a new tunnel they were driving into the pine log. This activity proved so interesting that when the teacher finally explained that my punishment was over and I could return to my seat, I couldn't believe my ears. I wasn't being punished, I was having a grand time and wanted to stay where I was. When I didn't budge, she came over to me, got a good grip on my shirt collar, and hauled me back to my seat. The whole business was pretty unreasonable and high-handed on her part, I thought, and our relationship had a more down-to-earth quality from then on.

Still, I liked her and thought she was about the smartest person in the whole county, except for my mother and father, of course. On the long walks across the prairie to and from school, Iris and I often talked confidentially with Grace, asking her advice about things we didn't understand or were worried about. One day when Iris had stayed home for some reason and there were just the two of us, I confessed that I was still having fears about the comet. I was very offhand about it, fearing she might laugh at me, but she didn't. She even tried to explain something about comets and how there had been many others before this one, and no one had been poisoned *yet*. And also how the sun and moon and millions of stars and other worlds were flying around up in the sky, and none had ever collided with us *yet*. But she only left me with the uneasy thought that even if they hadn't crashed into us or poisoned everybody *yet,* no one seemed positive that it couldn't happen. Though I had no definite idea when this calamity might occur, I was on a constant lookout for signs of its approach. Unusual cloud formations or sudden violent changes in the weather would inflame my fears and send my eyes racing across the fields and foothills toward the high mountains. I half expected to see a thick green cloud roll over their jagged peaks and, spreading out over the peaceful prairie, cover us all with silent death.

Later in the fall, when all the crops were finally harvested and the threshing finished, my sixteen-year-old cousin Joe could be spared from the ranch work to return to school and finish the eighth grade. Because of his age and size, he bullied us younger kids and teased us a lot. He soon learned of my fears about the comet and would make sly remarks to me. "Enjoy your Thanksgiving dinner, Mick," he said the day before that holiday. "It'll probably be your last one." Or maybe, on a zero morning when I was stamping around complaining about my frozen feet, he would say, "Quit whining about your feet; you won't need them much longer anyway." Somehow he decided, and it seemed very logical to me, that the world would come to an end at daybreak on Christmas morning.

As the winter deepened and December 25 approached, I became more and more uncertain and confused. Christmas was the most wonderful day of the year of course, but my normal impatience for its arrival continually collided with the horrible fear that when that day did come, it might also be my last. I didn't say anything about it because no one else seemed the least bit worried about the comet, and I knew from past experience that they would only make fun of me. And also, my own common sense had almost convinced me that Joe was a liar and I a fool to listen to him. Still, maybe those newspapermen were right. They had probably been to college and knew things we didn't know. The last couple of weeks I wavered back and forth between helpless dread and happy expectation.

Luckily, I was kept so busy that I didn't have much time for worrying. It was only in the cheerless grey light of early morning, while I lay "balled-up" under the warm, homemade comforters, waiting for the last bit of my mother's patience to run out before getting up, that my fears returned in full force.

School started as usual every morning, but as the day wore on, our reading, 'riting, and 'rithmetic disappeared under a flood of rehearsals for the play, practice for the Christmas carols, and work on our costumes.

One evening Frank and Grace left for a visit with Aunt Minnie, but the next morning the two school blackboards were covered with beautiful Christmas scenes done in colored chalk. We suspected them, but since we knew that neither of them could draw worth a hoot, we were mystified as to who the artist really was. Grace later confessed that she had brought with her from home large sheets of paper perforated with holes that outlined these scenes and a box of colored chalk. The paper was held against the blackboard and gently patted with an eraser well-filled with powdered milk. It was then a simple matter to fill in the dotted lines with the bright colors, adding a bit of gay charm to our small, dismal schoolroom.

Frank rode into the schoolyard early one afternoon just before Christmas Eve, dragging behind him through the snow two small fir trees. The best one was set up for our Christmas tree, and the other we cut up for decorations. We spent the remaining two days making paper chains, threading popcorn and cranberries into long strings, and hanging evergreen branches above the blackboard doors, and windows.

Evenings at home we made greeting cards and simple presents and decorations for our own Christmas tree. I was pretty good at stringing cranberry chains with a needle and thread but was a complete loss when working with popcorn, because I ate all the big fluffy kernels and wound up with such a sorry-looking article that just about everyone agreed it was fit only for throwing into the kitchen fire.

Twice during this final week I had the same nerve-shattering nightmare about some huge shapeless mass that was trying to get me. It seemed to surround the house, and although I shut and locked the doors and windows, it oozed in thick streams through the keyholes and spread out through the rooms. Then hunting me down, it finally found me in my bed, cowering under the blankets, and began slowly to strangle me. I struggled and fought with this bodiless monster and finally woke up yelling and thrashing, only to discover that I had crawled so far under the bedding to escape the cold of my bedroom that I was slowly smothering.

I kept on hoping, though, that if the world did come to an end, it would wait until after I had opened my presents on Christmas morning. I just had to know if I'd gotten that magic lantern!

By eight o'clock Christmas Eve everyone from the surrounding ranches had arrived at the school. Torval, the bachelor homesteader who lived nearby and was shining up to the teacher, had come early and fired up the stove and lit the three coal-oil reflector lamps. As each family arrived, the barn lantern that had served as a heater under the bobsled blankets was brought in and hung on a nail high on the log walls.

I peeked out from behind the bedsheet curtains that enclosed the stage, and marveled at the change in our drab schoolroom. It didn't seem like the same place. The yellow lamplight softened the rough walls and shone on the fragrant evergreens and the brightly colored blackboard scenes. Our Christmas tree, draped with popcorn and cranberry strings and gaily colored paper chains, towered so high that the cardboard and lace angel standing on its top brushed the ridgepole. There were tiny candles set in shiny tin holders clipped to the branches, but everyone was so scared of fire they were never lighted. The room was filled with the comfortable voices and well-known faces of our relatives and neighbors, all dressed up in their best store clothes, the men freshly barbered and shaved, the women in homemade curls and bits of treasured jewelry.

The teacher stepped in front of the curtain and announced that the program was about to begin. She asked the men standing along the walls to turn down the lanterns so that the actors would show up better under the stage lighting. This was done, accompanied by much shushing throughout the audience and some nervous giggling from behind the stage. Finally the curtains were pulled back to reveal Helen, our oldest student, standing under our two bracket lamps, ready to start the entertainment.

She began in a high, slightly quavering voice, "Welcome to our friends and relatives. We, the pupils of Sheep Creek elementary school, wish to present a Christmas program for your pleasure. We will begin with a poem, 'The Night before Christmas,' recited by Miss Iris Shatraw." Helen had begun with a pale face and uncertain delivery but rapidly picked up speed, finished with a rush, and blushing furiously, bolted from the stage.

Iris then stepped out and went through the poem with all the confidence of a Sarah Bernhardt. There was thunderous applause, and after a rather confused and hurried curtsy, she turned and rushed from the stage to get a quick hug and kiss from Grace.

The program continued. Since there were so few of us, we all had several recitations and one or more parts in the different plays. This, added to our unreliable memories and stage fright, resulted in some badly fractured poems and strangely mixed-up dialogues, much to the embarrassment of Grace and the uninhibited delight of the audience.

As a finale, I, being the youngest boy, was to run out on stage and capture Santa Claus when he appeared with his sackful of toys at the end of the program. I had been well rehearsed beforehand, but always with Johnny Rappold or my cousin Joe as Santa, so I wasn't quite prepared for the real Saint Nick when he arrived. It was pretty dark, the lights having been turned way down, when he bounded out of the shadows and onto the stage. Only it wasn't the jolly little St. Nicholas of the poem that I had been led to expect but a huge, black, furry creature with great clumping hoofs. I stood rooted to the floor, too scared to move. Iris gave me a shove from behind and whispered loud and clear, "Go get him, stupid. He'll get away."

But I set my heels solidly and couldn't be budged. "That

ain't Santa," I said loudly. "That's a bear!"

Santa, of course, was my cousin Leo in a bearskin coat and boots and cotton whiskers—his idea of how St. Nick should be dressed.

Long after midnight, with the lilting rhythm of "Turkey in the Straw" still echoing in my ears and with the delicious feeling of a stomachful of cold chicken and chocolate layer cake, I stumbled along with the rest of the family to the bobsled and burrowed deep into the thick layer of straw that filled the sleighbox. The horses, their long winter coats tinted silver with frost and their minds set on getting back to the warm stable as soon as possible, started off with a jerk and headed across the snowy prairie at a fast trot. My mother, holding the bundled-up baby in her arms, sat up front with my father under a big, hairy buffalo robe and happily gossiped about everyone at the party. My two sisters, twined together for warmth, disappeared under the heavy wool blanket that covered us. Frank and Grace sat at the very back of the bob with their shoulders and heads close together, talking softly.

Left to myself, I looked out across the frozen white world and suddenly remembered about tomorrow and the comet. Under the brilliant half moon hanging just above the western peaks, the smooth, glistening snow-covered prairie spread out in every direction, unmarked except for the occasional jackrabbit trails that crisscrossed it in ruler-straight lines. It looked to me as it had always looked on a moonlit night in deep winter. Then I noticed the long, low bank of clouds off to the north, stretching all the way from Harte Butte to the Sweetgrass Hills. My heart skipped a beat, and I watched it narrowly to see if it was coming any closer or getting any higher in the sky. But it didn't seem to be, and I sleepily decided that maybe it was just a storm coming up out of Canada after all.

"Wake up! Wake up, Mick!" Grace was shaking me gently, and I opened my eyes and saw we were home. As I stumbled across the footbridge and up the path to the house, I noticed the moon had set behind the mountains, leaving them standing close and black against the steel-blue sky. And off to the north, the long black cloud had climbed high above the valley's rim.

There was something ominous about it, but I couldn't remember what it was. Somehow I reached the house, and someone helped me to get undressed and into bed. But there was still something I was supposed to remember. . . .

I woke with a start, one instant completely dead to the world, the next everything crystal clear. It was after daylight, I knew automatically, though the room was still in deep gloom. My eyes darted to the window and I saw the snow falling, thick and quiet. Then I heard the rattle of stovelids and the clack of the pump and water splashing in the sink. I sat up with a jerk. It was Christmas morning, and everything was just as it should be. A great wave of happiness flowed over me. I kicked the bedclothes off onto the floor and dashed barefooted out of the bedroom, across the corner of the living room, and slid to a stop just inside the kitchen door. My father, a red-hot stove-lid on its lifter in one hand and a stick of stovewood in the other, looked at me over his shoulder. My mother stopped pumping water into the teakettle in midstroke. She too looked at me over her shoulder. They glanced at each other and smiled that certain kind of smile, then turned back to me and said almost in unison, "Merry Christmas, Mick!"

The Woollies

EARLY IN 1909 my father figured out a way to get rich or, at least, reasonably well-to-do. He decided that raising sheep—"woollies" as the cattlemen contemptuously called them—was the answer to our money problems and the sooner he got started the better. He was discussing it with my mother one blustery evening in the early spring, as we sat around the kitchen table after supper. Although he was a true optimist, he didn't go into things blindly. The table was littered with books and pamphlets about sheep raising, which he had been collecting and studying the past winter.

"Hell, Peg," he said to my mother, "we aren't getting anywhere raising cattle. That bunch I sold last year brought less than eight cents a pound delivered in Chicago. If I didn't have the money the threshing machine brought in last fall, we'd be way behind right now."

He stared in disgust at the scattered columns of figures he had worked out on the blue-lined scratch pad. I was watching with admiration the quick, easy way he could add and subtract and multiply. Anybody who could do that could certainly make money raising some dumb sheep. Besides, it would be new and exciting, and I was all for it.

But I could see that my mother wasn't entirely sold on the idea. Like me, she had confidence in my father, but her native cockney shrewdness demanded a lot of convincing.

"You don't know anything about sheep raising," she objected.

"I know. But I've been studying these all winter." His wave took in the scattered literature on the table. "And they all claim a climate such as we have here in Montana is the best in the world for raising Merino sheep. Nate Howe has promised to work for me steady for the first year, and he's an old hand with sheep.

"Besides," he went on, "there's always a lot of new homesteads filed on every year around here, and now with everyone going for dry-land farming, the open range that's left will soon be gone. How are you going to raise beef then? A Hereford steer will starve on the same amount of land that'll fatten a dozen sheep. It doesn't seem as if we have much choice."

Half convinced, my mother nodded in agreement. "All right. But let's go slow. Try it out easy so as not to get too deep in debt."

"Sure, sure," he agreed absently. "Now, let's see. You know that desert land you filed on last year? There's a dry, level spot up there that's just right to build the new sheep shed on."

My mother sprang to her feet. "What sheep shed?" she yelled. "And how much will that cost?"

But my father waved his hands soothingly. "Not much, Peg, honest. We'll pay for it easy with the first shearing."

She was far from satisfied. "We'll probably wind up in the poorhouse," she prophesied darkly as she rounded up the little kids and started getting them ready for bed.

By early May the fences were mended and the crops planted, so my father put my cousin Frank and Old Man Moon to digging the forty postholes necessary for framing the sheep shed. I hurried home from school that first day they worked on it and went straight to the building site to see how much was done. The two men, sweaty and disgusted, were sitting on a long pole, surveying the dirt piles that marked the few holes they had dug that day.

"Gosh, you didn't get many holes dug," I observed, "What you been doing anyway?"

Frank grabbed me and knuckled my uncut hair with his fist until I yelled. "Smart-alec," he growled.

"Cut it out, Frank," Old Moon ordered. "He's just a little kid."

I pulled free and laughed. I didn't really mind. Frank was my best friend, and I knew he hadn't meant to hurt.

"Uncle Ed couldn't have picked a worse place to build his damn shed," Frank complained. "I never saw so many rocks in one place in my whole life."

"Pa says it's always dry up here and sheep like that."

"Guess he's picked a sheep heaven then," Moon said. "If these rocks were flat, the whole place would be paved. It's going to be a tough job to get all those holes dug."

"Well, that's what we get paid for," Frank said as he struggled to his feet, spit on his hands, and picked up the crow bar. "Come on, Moon, supper's still two hours away."

In spite of Frank's griping and old Moon's doubts, the holes were dug and the poles set—all forty of them.

Meanwhile my father had been busy figuring the sizes and amounts of lumber needed and hauling them from the sawmill. The shingles had to come from the lumberyard and were pretty expensive, so he was careful not to let my mother find out how much that big roof was going to cost.

He was a practical carpenter and a good planner, and the building went up at an amazing rate. Leo, Frank's brother, and Cliff, one of our young neighbors, were hired to help out. Carpentry was a change in the ranch routine, and the boys looked on it almost as fun. They often went back to the unfinished shed after supper, working until stopped by darkness. I could help some, too, picking up lumber scraps, running errands, holding one end of a board till it was nailed in place, so I felt like one of the crew. Actually, though, I was usually underfoot and in the way—like the time I was heartily sworn at by Leo for ruining a freshly sharpened saw by sawing halfway through a ten-penny nail.

One morning after the June rains were over and the road dry enough to carry a good load, my father put the extra-high box on the lumber wagon and hitched one of his heavy teams to it. He then harnessed another team and tied them to the tail-gate of the wagon. "The road is still soft in places, and we'll need a four-horse team to pull that load of shingles home," he said as he tossed an extra set of eveners and a short log chain aboard.

I climbed over the wagon wheel and on up to the wide spring seat, where I got a good hold on the iron rail that ran around its side and across the back. The seat of my pants was about eight feet from the ground, and the road rutty and full of rocks, so no one had to tell me to hang on.

We reached town well before noon and pulled up alongside the lumberyard. My father got out his list and went inside. In a few minutes two men came out and put a keg of shingle nails and some odds and ends of lumber in the wagon, then started piling in the bundles of shingles. They piled and piled until the wagon was filled almost to overflowing. When the last one was in place and my father had climbed onto the seat, I said to him, "Boy! I bet they cost a lot of money."

He looked a little guilty for a second, then recovered his usual assurance. "Shucks, Mick," he said. "We can buy ten loads like this with our first lamb crop." I knew he was the smartest man in Teton County, so I quit worrying.

We drove the wagon into the shade of a nearby cottonwood tree, unhitched and fed the horses, then crossed over to Harris Brothers' store. My father went over the grocery list with Sam

Harris and looked over his assortment of axes. After much heft-
ing and false swinging, he decided on a double-bitted one that
hung just right. He also had Sam set out a pail of axle grease
and, just as we were leaving, remembered to add the five-gallon
can of coal oil that my mother had forgotten to put on the list.

By now I was starving, and so was my father, I guess, for he
headed straight for the hotel and dinner. But as we were passing
the saloon, my father looked over the half-doors and stopped
short.

"There's Nate Howe," he said. "Just the man I want to see.
He ought to have some sheep located for me by now. You wait;
I'll be out in a minute."

Half way through the doors he stopped and looked back.
"You pretty hungry, Mick?" he asked.

"I sure am!" I said.

"We-l-ll, come in with me; guess it won't hurt you any this
once."

I had never been in a saloon before, but I had often peeked
under the high swinging doors on other trips to town. I took in
everything as I followed him across the wide, unpainted, and
not too clean floor. Several round tables circled by low-backed
armchairs filled one side of the room, and a pool table stood in
the corner. The highly varnished bar, guarded by a brightly
polished foot rail, ran the full length of the opposite wall. The
long shelf in back, except for the space taken up by a broad,
gilt-framed mirror, was piled high with bottles of all shapes,
sizes, and colors.

Nate Howe, a small man with a battered tan hat and an
oversized jumper, was in the act of downing a healthy swig of
draft beer. At the sound of our clumsy shoes pounding across
the bare floor, he looked at us over his shoulder. Setting the
half-empty mug carefully on the bar, he wiped his mouth with
his sleeve and said, "Hello, Ed. Just the man I want to see.
What'll you have?"

It seemed to me that the best way to find someone in this
town was to hang around in the saloons.

"Got any coffee?" my father asked. "And how about a sand-

wich?" The bartender nodded, then looked at me. "How about
the boy?" he said.

"Oh, give him the best in the house," my father answered
offhandedly as he turned to Nate. Nate was a great tobacco
chewer, and even though he was drinking beer, I could see a big
cud tucked away up in his left cheek. He grinned at me, showing a lot of yellow teeth behind his scrubby mustache. "Hello,
Mick," he said. "Hanging around saloons already? Wait till
your Ma hears about this!"

I looked at my father, and he gave me a big wink.

"About the sheep, Ed." Nate turned back to my father.
"There's a man the other side of Shelby who . . . ," and the men
went on making plans about buying sheep.

I stood looking over the display of bottles behind the bar
and wondered which one was best. Dan, the bartender, came
back in a few minutes with my father's coffee and sandwich.
The he looked at me and scratched his head and finally reached
under the bar to pull out a quart bottle of strawberry soda. He
set it on the counter in front of me, adding from the lunch
counter a bowl filled with oyster crackers, two hard-boiled eggs,
and some huge dill pickles. My father noticing that they were
too high for me to reach, picked me up and set me on the bar.
Dan laughed. "Get going, Mick! It's all yours," he said as he
popped the cork and filled a beer glass with the sparkling pink
liquid.

Ten minutes later the cracker bowl was empty, and I was
drinking the last glass of soda pop. I was comfortably full, and
except for the soda backfiring a lot, making my nose tingle and
my eyes water, I felt fine. My father sure knew his business
when he ordered the best in the house for me.

Sometime later the heavy wagon with its four-horse hitch
lumbered across the new bridge over Dupuyer Creek and
headed into the afternoon sun toward home, ten miles to the
west.

One of my unfulfilled dreams was driving a four-horse
team, and now seemed a good time to proposition my father
about it. But he shook his head, while keeping a steady eye on

the horses. "You've got to be strong and hold the lines just so," he said, demonstrating with his hands. "Keep the leaders moving fast and hold a tight rein on the wheelers. If the two teams get too close together and get tangled in each other's gear, you're got a hell of a mess on your hands, maybe a runaway even. Nope, you'll have to wait a while, Mick."

He had hinted that it would be just as well not to mention our lunch at the saloon when we got home, but I couldn't resist bragging that night to Frank that I had actually sat on the saloon bar and drunk pink soda. My mother just laughed, though, and said it was all right as long as I stuck to soda and kept away from the pool table.

The following Saturday we had our shingling bee, and several of the neighboring families came—the men to lay shingles, the women to help with dinner, the kids to have fun. One thing about our bees was that whether it was for a house raising, a threshing, or a shingling, the job was a serious, no-fooling-around affair. By early afternoon the last shingle was laid and the ridgeboards nailed in place. Now we were ready for dinner, which was served up in our kitchen with a generous hand, well spiced with comfortable talk and uninhibited laughter.

It had been a rainy spring, and we had an especially heavy stand of hay to cut and stack. Several violent thunderstorms during July slowed the haying down until my father began to worry about whether he would be through by the time the sheep arrived. He knew he would have to leave on his threshing round early in September, and any work connected with the sheep would have to be finished by that time. Long hours of work and some final cooperation by the weather resulted in his having the last haystack topped off by mid-August. Two days later the sheep, all twelve hundred of them, were delivered by Jeff, the burly French-Canadian herder who worked for us off and on for as long as we had sheep.

The sheep ate steadily all the time and still never seemed to get enough. Our natural grass, or buffalo grass, cured on the stalk in our dry climate and could be eaten all winter. Cattle, horses, and sheep fared very well even in deep winter by pawing

the snow away and eating the exposed dried grass; so the grazing near the ranch had to be saved for the winter months when
the sheep could be penned up nightly, safe from the weather in
our big shed. For this reason, almost as soon as he arrived with
the sheep, Jeff started driving them to the northern range, several miles away. There my father built a temporary corral with
fenceposts and sheep panels, and set up a small tent nearby for
the herder, complete with grub, cooking utensils, firewood, and
bedroll.

We soon found out that sheep were so dumb they were always getting into trouble. They fell in badger holes and broke
their legs, ate locoweed and lost what few brains they might
have once possessed. Sometimes they could be stampeded by a
flash of lightning or the sight of a startled jackrabbit, and
would run till they fell over a cutbank or piled up along a line
fence and trampled one another to death by the dozens. So
there had to be a full-time herder, assisted by a good dog or two,
to watch over them by day and to make sure they were securely
locked up at night. Even then if the herder left them too long, a
pair of marauding coyotes could jump the fence and kill or
maim fifty sheep in a few minutes of senseless slaughter. A sheepherder didn't have to be too bright, but he did have to be trust-
worthy, able to live for weeks with only himself and his dog for
company, and he had to know some of the rudiments of veteri-
nary practice. Jeff was an old, reliable hand with the woollies,
but Melvin, who substituted one year while Jeff was on his "vacation," nearly put us out of the sheep business.

Melvin, a nephew of Nate Howe, was a divinity student back East. He had contracted some kind of lung sickness
and was having a slow recovery. He wrote his aunt in early summer to say that his doctor had advised him to find some light
work in a high, dry climate. Our Montana sheep ranch, where
he could sit on a hillside, soaking up fresh air and sunshine
while watching a few gentle sheep, would be just the right place
for him, she thought. My father had his doubts about Melvin as
a sheepherder, and started to object, but when Mrs. Howe
broke into noisy sobs and my mother backed her up by throw-

ing some dirty looks his way, he hastily agreed to hire Melvin.

We were all on the porch one hot afternoon, loafing for a while before going back to haying, when the Howes drove up with Melvin. My father slowly stiffened in his chair as he watched them cross the footbridge and start up the path. Mrs. Howe was in the lead, closely followed by Melvin while Nate straggled along behind them, lugging a bulging suitcase. Melvin was something of a sight. I leaned forward for a better look, and so did everyone else. He was about twenty, I guessed, long and hungry-looking, and with the uncertain gate of a new-born colt. Everyone in Teton County was thoroughly tanned by this time of the year, so Melvin's dead-white hands and face were a shock to us, contrasting as they did with his rusty black suit and shiny black waistcoat buttoned high under his chin. He apparently had eye trouble as well as lung trouble, for he squinted out from behind small, steel-rimmed glasses. A wide-brimmed, low-crowned hat topped off the costume of this unlikely hired hand.

My father sat speechless at first, then managed to blurt out in a hoarse whisper, "My God, Peg! I didn't hire *that* to herd sheep, did I?"

"Shut up, Ed!" she whispered back. "They'll hear you. And don't forget, he's practically a minister, so watch your language."

That night at the bunkhouse I joined Frank and Nolan in their raucous laughter; and even Old Moon, who was a little obsessed with religion himself, couldn't repress an occasional smile when we talked Melvin over. Still later my feelings of disdain turned to active dislike when my mother told me that Melvin was to have my bed that night and I was to sleep on a folded comforter in a corner of the living room floor.

"You can't expect a real minister to sleep in the bunkhouse," she said. "There's no telling what those two hoodlums might say to him. And you can't expect him to sleep on the floor either."

I couldn't make sense out of what my mother was saying, since for the next few weeks Melvin was going to sleep on the

cold ground with only a blanket and a ground sheet under him.
I never did get very far arguing with my mother, though; she
always settled the discussion by ordering me to "shut up, and
do as I tell you!"

We had a little trouble getting Melvin up in time to go to
the sheep camp with us the next morning. It took some restrained swearing by my father and some kindly advice from my
mother to convince him that sheepherding had to start well before ten o'clock; in fact, daylight was the time to get up and
start the sheep on their day's grazing.

We reached camp by eight o'clock and found the sheep
fanned out and well up the flank of a high butte off to the west.
Jeff had finished his breakfast and was putting the tent to rights,
for he was a very neat tentkeeper. He greeted me with a loud
"How's Mick?" and a slap across the backside that raised me a
foot off the ground and brought tears to my eyes, convincing me
that we were still the best of friends. My father introduced Melvin and explained that he would take over the sheep for a couple of weeks while Jeff went to town and "enjoyed himself." Jeff
shook his head in a dazed sort of way, and even though he had
been on the range a long while and was anxious to leave, he
suggested, "Maybe I'd better hang around for a day or two 'til
Melvin gets used to the woollies." My father looked relieved
and quickly agreed that that was a good idea.

They all three walked off talking sheep, leaving me behind
to examine the broken-winged hawk that Jeff had found and
brought home to doctor. The hawk was tethered to his perch in
front of the tent and sat quietly as I slowly walked around him,
except that he continuously turned his head, following me with
his hard yellow eyes. After the fifth circuit, I was astonished he
hadn't wrung his own neck.

I was still trying to solve the puzzle when the men came
back, so I asked Jeff about it. "Damned if I know, Mick," he
said. "The other day I made fifty trips around him—I kept
count—and nothing happened. He must have a spring or something in his neck."

Melvin laughed, giggled really, and explained, "He just

turns his head half-way around, then snaps it back the other way so fast you can't see him do it. He could keep it up all day." This seemed reasonable, and I was impressed. Maybe Melvin wasn't quite as stupid as he looked.

We went home later in the day, but my father was pretty uneasy about Melvin. He complained to my mother that night, "I don't think that parson has a brain in his head. I would rather trust Mick, here. And maybe that's what I'd better do, let Mick work them while Jeff's away."

I didn't like the way the talk was going. Last year Chief Salois had seen grizzly tracks right up there in that neighborhood. I didn't like sheep well enough to fight a coyote over them, let alone a grizzly bear. But my mother came to my rescue. "Don't talk nonsense, Ed!" she sputtered. "Melvin will be all right. You just wait and see."

"Damn it, Peg!" my father swore, "I'm not worried about Melvin; I'm worried about my sheep!"

Jeff came by late the next afternoon to change his clothes and head for town and his first, long-awaited drink. He shook his head dolefully at my father and wondered aloud if there would be any sheep left for him to herd when he got back.

"Don't you think he'll make out?" my father asked.

Jeff laughed, "Maybe Melvin knows all about taking care of souls, but he sure don't know a damn thing about looking after sheep." And he swung briskly off down the lane.

My father decided not to visit the sheep camp right away, agreeing to my mother's demand that Melvin be given a fair chance to prove himself on his new job. But on the second morning, after explaining to us at breakfast that he'd better go see if Melvin needed anything, he saddled up Snort and rode hurriedly off across the prairie. Frank and old Moon hitched up the hay wagon to draw in the last of the hay from the old Bergland place while Nolan raked. I went along to drive. We brought in two loads that morning and were just crossing the bridge on our way to dinner when we saw my father coming across the flats. Snort was sweat-stained and coming along at a swinging lope, which was mighty fast traveling for my father who was no slap-dash cowboy.

"Oh, oh," Frank said. "Looks like trouble!" And we turned back to the wagon yard to wait for him.

My father was giving out orders even as he stepped down from the saddle. "Frank, get your horse saddled right after dinner. We've got to go out and round up those sheep. That Melvin's got them scattered to hell and gone, and I only hope we can get them rounded up again by dark. Nolan, you and Moon try to get the rest of that hay in; it looks like rain tomorrow."

We ate a hurried dinner, and between mouthfuls my father related this morning's troubles.

"When I got over to the camp," he said, "Melvin had about two hundred sheep in a tight band and was holding them. I asked where the rest of them were, and he started to cry. Said he didn't know. That they had gotten scattered yesterday, and except for the few we could see, the rest were lost.

"I rode to the top of a hill and could see them off to the west but broken up into three or four small bands. I tried to bunch them, but they're pretty nervous and ready to run. Maybe they'll quiet down, and when we get back, we can get them together."

Then he turned to me and continued, "Get your shoes on, Mick; you can help. You ride over double with Frank, and then bring his horse back tonight. Frank's going to have to stay with the sheep until Jeff gets back. And Melvin's going back to his aunt's where he belongs"—this last with an I-told-you-so look at my mother, who looked meekly at her plate and pretended not to hear him.

Frank would do almost anything for my father, even herd sheep. But he griped about it to me all the way over to the north range. "I never thought I'd wind up a crazy sheepherder!" he said "Not even for Uncle Ed. And that Jeff had better get back pretty soon, or I'll take off for Canada and to hell with the sheep!" We both knew this was just a lot of talk, and I didn't pay much attention because I was thinking how I was going to ride Frank's long-legged cow pony, Star, home that night, and with a saddle, too.

At the end of a long afternoon of running up and down gullies, through buckbrush, and across prickly pear patches, Melvin and I on foot and the others mounted, we managed to get all the sheep together and in their pen before dark.

"I'll be over for you in the morning with the buckboard," my father told Melvin, choking back the string of cusswords he ordinarily used at times like this. "I don't think you were cut out for a sheepherder!" he finished grimly.

Melvin's eyes filled with tears. "I never thought sheep could be so difficult," he said. "I always thought they were gentle and easy to handle."

Frank and I howled with laughter at these sentimental ideas about sheep, but my father just shook his head in disbelief and said, not unkindly, "Melvin, I'm afraid you've got a lot to learn about a lot of things. And especially about sheep."

Every year after the spring lambing was over, the buck sheep were kept separated from the ewes until well into November, in order to bring the lambing season mostly in the month of May. Our buck pasture was a ten-acre lot enclosed with a woven wire fence. This was normally large enough to provide forage for our thirty or so rams. Sometimes, if the lot was being shifted to provide extra grazing during a dry spell, they were herded into the corral for a few days. This crowding, along with their enforced celibacy, didn't help their dispositions any and resulted in more than the usual amount of fighting among them. When a duel was on, the two bucks would face each other, standing about fifty feet apart, their big curved horns ready, while the rest of the band formed a circle of interested spectators. On some kind of unseen signal, they charged toward each other at full speed and ended the run with a spectacular leap that brought the two heads together with a resounding *crack*. They would bounce back after each collision to stand, stiff-legged and groggy, waiting for renewed energy to continue the fight. Either their few brains were well protected, or they didn't have any at all. Frank and I bet on the no-brains theory, for they could go through this ordeal several times without much visible damage. Eventually, one would weaken and go down, to be unmercifully battered by the watchers until he finally dragged himself off into a corner to recover. Every year these bouts took place until the boss of the herd was decided, after which he proceeded to keep order, dealing out swift punishment to all upstarts.

Old Pie-Eye was one of the these chiefs who became so mean that he finally wound up as mutton stew, and mighty tough eating he was, too. Pie-Eye got his name because in one of his many battles his left eye was so badly damaged that it became fixed in a wild stare, blind and useless. He was ready at all times to pick a fight, and whether it was with a five-pound Plymouth Rock rooster or a half-ton Hereford steer didn't seem to matter to him.

Teasing Pie-Eye until he chased me out of the corral was one of my favorite sports, and it had the added thrill of a probable licking if my father caught me. The old buck finally cured me of this pastime in his own thorough fashion. One afternoon the family drove over to the Howes' for a visit, leaving me at home with Louis St. Denis, who was visiting for a few days. We had the ranch to ourselves and soon got into a dare game with old Pie-Eye. Our idea was to see who could get closest to him and still beat him to the fence when he charged. On the last run he suddenly picked up speed, and I never had a chance. Louis was a little older than I and faster on his feet, so he made it to safety. Just before I reached the fence, Pie-Eye hit me, and when I came to my senses, I was flat on my back on the other side of the corral fence with Louis pouring creek water from his hat onto my face. He had been so busy climbing the fence, he didn't see what happened to me, and I couldn't remember for sure whether I went under, over, or through the fence. We judged that from the size of the bump on my head and the ripped-up state of my clothes, I must have gone through the rails. I lied to my mother that night, claiming I had fallen down the haychute into the manger, accounting for my battered condition.

A few days later my father was repairing the latch on the barn door, which opened into the corral. He had his back to the sheep and was busily working when some survival instinct caused him to look around. The old boss sheep was headed straight for him. Just as the buck made his final leap my father dodged and Pie-Eye crashed through the door, tearing it from its hinges and scattering broken boards half way across the stable. After surveying the damage, my father, realizing how dangerous the animal could be, went to the house, got his rifle, and shot Old Pie-Eye dead on the spot.

While sheep had some good points, there were a lot of things about them that none of us liked. For one thing, wool is oily. When you had to handle sheep a lot, such as at lambing and shearing times, your clothes collected a thick layer of grease that smelled like the floor of a well-used sheep shed. My mother battled this grease and smell on our clothes with fierce determination, cursing the thick scum left by our hard water and forcing me to spend many agonizing hours slaving at the washing machine. The smell persisted, however, though she tried to make the men change their workclothes before coming into the house after a session in the barn or sheep shed.

Even so, when my Aunt Annie, who was kind of finicky, came from Helena to visit us, she always complained about the animal smell around the house.

"I don't know how you stand it," she said one time. "The men always smell like a horse barn or sheep shed."

"Well, it never hurt me any!" my mother answered tartly. Then she snickered and asked, "Maybe you'd like to hear what the hired men say about you?"

Aunt Annie stared expectantly at her. (I was sitting in my father's armchair, supposedly reading but actually listening avidly to the conversation.)

"They say that you smell—" she hesitated, looked at me, then lowered her voice, "that you use the same perfume as the 'girls across the tracks.' "

Aunt Annie was speechless for a moment, then broke into her familiar hoarse laughter and finally gasped, "Well, ain't that something!" She and my mother continued to giggle uncontrollably, but I couldn't see where there was any joke. I always thought Aunt Annie smelled beautiful.

Another thing I hated was sheep ticks. They looked like tiny reddish crabs and had clutching feet and a bite like an alligator's. They tended to congregate under your belt and between your legs, and when they gave you a nip on your more tender parts, it could raise you right off the ground. They seemed to thrive on the sheep dip that was supposed to kill them, so we always had a good supply of them.

When a lamb was born, both mother and baby were brought from the range in a covered wagon and put in a small private pen up in the sheep shed. There they were carefully tended for several days to protect them against disease and accident. Occasionally an ewe would reject her new-born lamb, and even kill it if they were not separated, so it might be fobbed off on another mother whose baby had died. The foster mother would ordinarily welcome the waif and adopt it, but sometimes a little scheming was necessary to help things along. One of the tricks Nate Howe showed us was to skin the dead lamb and put the hide on the orphan. This nearly always worked, since the stupid mother was quite satisfied if the lamb smelled right. But there were always a couple of orphans that no sheep would adopt, as well as a few sickly ones that needed special nursing, and these were brought down to the house to be raised by hand.

By the end of the lambing season each of us kids had a pet lamb or two, and it was up to us to feed them cow's milk twice a day, using an old whisky bottle equipped with a rubber baby's nipple. They grew very fast and could soon give you quite a tussle. They were playful as puppies and enjoyed rough-housing as much as we did. It seemed no time until they were eating grass and grain, and the milk became a sort of dessert, which they gorged down happily. Finally, the day came when my father stood by the pen, eyeing them with satisfaction, and pronounced judgment, "They aren't lambs any more. They're sheep." The next day we kids sadly drove them out to the lane to join the main herd as it went by, headed for the day's grazing.

The young lambs, except for the ones that became pets,

were kept with their mothers and divided into small bands of a hundred or so, according to age, to graze by themselves. As a result we had several of these small bands scattered around the ranch, each with its own pen and temporary shelter. I was supposed to keep them from getting mixed up during the day and to lock them up in their own pen at night.

Every evening we counted the lambs and ewes to be sure they came out even. If a lamb was missing, we started searching, usually finding it deep in a late afternoon nap in the shade of a sagebush or stuck in a badger hole calmly waiting to be rescued. When the count was right, the next job was to make sure all the children were fed. This was easy. We just examined any lamb that was blatting his head off, and if his stomach was flat, we knew he had had no supper. Then we had to find the neglectful mother, catch her, throw her flat, and hold her while the lamb filled up. At the age of nine or ten, a boy is about an even match for a full-grown ewe. At first I got dragged all over the prairie, through rockpiles and prickly-pear patches, but eventually I became a fairly good wrestler, familiar with the old reliable holds (plus a few dirty ones I figured out for myself), and so was able to perform my nursing job to my father's satisfaction.

The first few days of my sheepherding were all right. There were things to watch—the birds, the jackrabbits, and antics of the young lambs. I could often coax one of my sisters or young brothers to spend part of the day with me. But as time went on, it became more difficult to find company until even my trusted friend, Monday, would sneak off looking for something more exciting to do. I was always glad when the sheep were all together again and the regular herder in charge of them. There was something scary about being alone so much, and I didn't like it. I certainly didn't want to start talking to myself and acting funny so that people would call me a "crazy sheepherder."

The shearing crew arrived in late June or early July, and this was the beginning of an exciting week for me. These dozen or so young men traveled from ranch to ranch, wherever there were sheep. They were a husky lot for it took a good man to work at high speed in a shearing pen through a ten-hour day. They were paid by the number of pounds of wool they clipped, and each man was determined to make a few more dollars than anyone else. There was also a deep sense of rivalry that lasted throughout the season as to who was the best shearer in the band. The men, stripped to the waist, worked at top speed, the sweat dripping from their glistening bodies and the bright steel blades of the shears shining out in the gloom of the shed as they were driven into the matted wool. As I walked along, reluctantly offering drinking water I had laboriously carried up from the house, I felt the excitement in the air. Each man toiled to cut a few extra pounds of wool, to become top man for that day or to win a private bet with a rival. Moving about, I was able to keep a rough check in my head, passing the word as to how each man was doing and openly cheering for the man I liked best.

Just before shearing time we built a series of small temporary pens down the center of our big sheep shed, each having a low platform across one end where the actual shearing was done. Every morning two dozen sheep were put in each pen, and the men, working in pairs, climbed in. The shearer grabbed the sheep nearest him, dragging it to the platform and shoving it down into a sitting position. Without loss of motion, he began cutting off the long wool, starting at the animal's head and snipping around its body in narrow hands until the coat was free and lay on the floor in one complete pelt. My father weighed each fleece after it was tied into a neat bundle and credited it to the proper shearer. He also examined every sheep as it emerged pale yellow and naked-looking, and doctored up the nicked skin and ocassional deep gash inflicted by a careless or clumsy worker. The men crowded around him at the end of the day as he totaled up the tally sheet and announced each man's poundage. There was a lot of good-natured arguing and horseplay as the bets were settled up and new ones made for the next day.

Aside from carrying water, I also carried the bundles of

wool to the far end of the shed, where a ten-foot-long burlap
sack hung with gaping mouth from a high pole platform. Every
so often I climbed a ladder to this platform, and my father
tossed the bundles up to me and I dropped them into the sack.
From time to time, as the bag filled up, I would climb down
into it, jumping around and packing it tight. This was a lot of
fun, though I did end up each night greasy, dirty, sweaty, and
crawling with sheep ticks.

Each day my mother struggled with the work of feeding
this crew of ravenous eaters. Usually Mrs. Howe or Nettie
Pfeiffer would come and help out with the unbelievable amount
of cooking and washing of dishes there was to do. They
prepared, cooked, and served a whole sheep and a bushel of potatoes, baked a dozen loaves of bread, and brewed gallons of
coffee each day the shearers were there. On the last day she always had hot dried-apple pie, generously smothered in
whipped cream, as a sort of celebration that the shearing was
over and she had a full year ahead to rest up for the next one.

For me, the best time was after supper each night. The
men congregated in front of the bunkhouse, some washing and
shaving or cutting one another's hair. Others didn't give a damn
how they looked or smelled. They just lounged around, swap-
ping lies and opinions about horses and people—all of which
were highly seasoned with profanity, of course,.

But there was one job they all did without fail, and that
was to sharpen their sheep shears.

A sheep, in the year's time between shearings, could pick
up an amazing amount of sand and gravel in his greasy coat,
which could quickly dull even the hardest steel. So my father's
patent emery wheel got a good workout each evening as each
man roughground his two pairs of shears on it, after which he
honed them to a razor's edge on his own private oilstone.

By the time these chores were out of the way, the sun had
dropped behind the jagged fence of mountains to the west, and
the evening air had turned cool. Mosquitoes appeared by the
thousands, all looking for blood. A small campfire, built on the
bare ground of the wagon yard, took away some of the chill, and

if it smoked enough, it kept the mosquitoes at bay. It was also a cheerful place for everyone to get together that last hour before going to bed.

If my mother had had her way, I would never have been allowed within earshot of these sessions. "That's no place for a kid," she stormed. "Down there with that bunch of bums! Mick's too young."

But my father realized how much I wanted to be one of the gang and dug deep into his reserves of courage to stand up for me. "Hell, Peg," he said. "Mick's ten, and it's time he started to grow up. Besides he's hung around the hired men since he could walk; he's heard about everything by now, I imagine."

My mother gave her grudging assent with the understanding that my father or cousins would send me back to the house if the conversation became too raw. So I became part of the tight circle around the campfire, saying little but with my ears pricked up so as to miss nothing.

The evening usually started out mildly enough with talk of sheep, cattle, horses, and, of course, the neighbors. But gradually it worked into more interesting things such as Saturday nights in town with whisky drinking and poker playing and visits to "a certain house." About then one of my cousins would look at me and say, "Bedtime, Mick," and if I protested, he would pick me up by the shirt collar and march me across the footbridge.

I liked it best, though, when Nolan brought out his mandolin and, after a lot of plunking with his homemade pick, got it somewhat in tune. Then after a few preliminary chords, he would swing out with "Red River Valley," and we would all join in, following in the wake of Frank's strong baritone. At first we stuck to the old favorites and the latest song hits from back East, such as "Meet Me in St. Louie, Louie" and "Pony Boy." As the evening wore on, the entertainment picked up speed, and "The Old Grey Mare" and "Clementine" blossomed out with some very interesting and, to me, new verses. But when Nolan struck up his favorite windup song, "I Had a Girl Name Lulu," I was chased across the bridge and never learned any more about this lady except that "she wore a cotton frock."

After the shearers left, the entire flock of sheep was sent out on the range to fatten. Some would be shipped to Chicago in the late fall for slaughter; others—all the young and healthy ewes and a few rams—were kept through the winter as breeding stock for another year's crop.

We didn't really get started on the road to riches that year after all. With the cost of the new sheep shed and the interest on the bank loan (whatever that was), it was a good thing my father had the threshing rig to fall back on again. But he had learned a lot about sheep raising. In fact, we all had. He was sure that next year would be a lot better, but that year was to be disappointing too. A sudden flash of lightning one sultry day stampeded the fool sheep over a cutbank, and later we counted over a hundred of them lying dead in the stream below. And when our spring lambs and the summer's cut of wool reached the market, the prices were down. So once again the old J. I. C. threshing machine paid for the big box of clothing, household supplies, and Christmas presents that were ordered from Sears & Roebuck that fall.

One bitter cold night of the winter following our second year of sheep ranching, we were all sitting around the long kitchen table after supper, while the big cooking range chewed away hungrily, roaring a little in its throat and winking cheerfully at us through the joints in the firebox and stovelids. We kids were doing our hated homework, and my mother sat in her rocking chair under the lamp, working steadily at the mending in her overflowing basket.

For the past hour my father had been wrestling with his account book, shuffling through bills and canceled checks, chewing thoughtfully on his pencil as he compiled long columns of figures, frowning as he added and subtracted. Finally, he closed the book with a snap and looked around the pleasant lamp-lit room, then back at the bent heads of his busy family. Slowly the worried lines creasing his face disappeared, ironed out by the return of his usual optimistic smile. "You know, Peg," he announced cheerfully, "we didn't do so bad this year after all."

My mother looked up, then dropped the mending in her lap, and went to the heart of the situation in her usual direct way.

"How much money have we got in the bank?" she asked.

"Well, that ain't the point," he hedged. "We got the sheep paid for, and next year—"

"Of course," my mother broke in, starting to breathe fire. "It's always next year. The only way we'll ever get some real money in our hands is to sell out."

I had been half-heartedly trying to memorize the second stanza of "The Wreck of the Hesperus," my "language" lesson for the next day; but when I heard "sell out," I forgot all about school and sat stunned. Everyone talked about "selling out," but almost no one ever did, and I didn't see how my father could either. What would he do about Snort, and our dog Monday, and Jeff, and the sheep that were finally paid for? A big chunk of ice slid into my stomach when I thought of not seeing Frank and Leo every day, of never driving the hay wagon again or riding Old Dash after the milk cows on a warm summer evening. But somehow thoughts of things my mother had talked so much about crept slyly into my mind; civilization and Helena, "decent" houses, "decent" schools, ten-cent movies, and trolley rides. Maybe it would be kind of fun.

My father's voice broke through my thoughts, and I started listening again.

"Yes," he was saying to my mother, "there's been a lot in the papers lately about opening up the Peace River country." He was leaning forward in his chair, his blue eyes shining with excitement. "And I've been thinking that it would be a wonderful chance for a family like us to get a real start in life."

"Peace River?" my mother asked innocently. "Where's that?"

"It's up in northern Canada—" but he got no farther.

My mother leaped to her feet and glared across the table. "Northern Canada!" she exploded. "If you think I'm going to bury the children and myself in another godforsaken hole, you'd better think again. If we ever get back to civilization . . . "

and she was off under a full head of steam.

My father sat quietly, only half listening. His thoughts, it was easy to see, were still among the fresh new grainfields and the unspoiled rolling prairies of the far north. With a sigh of regret he turned his attention back to my mother and nodded absently, then he looked at me with a wink that said as plain as words, "Some other time, huh, Mick?"

Our Indian Neighbors

It always seemed to me that spring really arrived on the ranch when the first little band of Indian horsemen galloped by our log house. The Blackfoot Indians, just by passing by, brought excitement into our lives and left me with a never-satisfied curiosity about their families, their homes, and their activities. During the long, cold winters, when our road was empty of travelers, I thought often of the spring, which would bring back the Indians, especially Chief Four Horns and his fast-stepping sorrel team.

Out here the march of the prairie to the west is stopped short by the mile-high Rocky Mountains, which stretch north to south and act as a seasonal dam holding up the approach of the warm air from the Pacific. One day it suddenly breaks through, and spring flows down the western slopes, arriving with a nerve-tingling rush, bringing with it the early flowers, the flooding creek, the north-bound geese, and the reappearance of our Indian neighbors.

The winter I was nine years old was an especially hard one.

After months of bitter cold and driving snow, of biting winds
and frozen earth, I woke one morning and felt the change. The
air in my small bedroom had lost its nip, and outdoors the early
morning sunlight had turned from crystal to gold. It looked
warm again, and I bounced up in bed, poised for a dash
through the house and out the kitchen door for that first delicious smell of early spring. Then I heard a distant sound. I
stopped. I cocked my ear and held my breath. Now it came faint
but clear, slicing through the thick log walls and filling the
room with a wild clamor. Even before I had cleared the bedroom door on my mad rush to get outdoors, I was screaming,
"The geese are coming! The geese are here!"

I whizzed through the kitchen and banged open the outside
door, heading for the front yard. My mother was standing beside the kitchen range frying thick slices of bacon in a huge iron
skillet. She started her automatic, "Stop that—" then catching
the wild-goose call, she changed to an eager, "Wait for me!" and
shoving the half-cooked bacon back from the heat, she dashed
out behind me. We came to a stop in the middle of the front
yard, eagerly searching the southern sky for the first glimpse of
the birds. Finally we located them, a long, thin, flickering line
just clearing the valley's rim and heading straight for us.

When they had gone south last fall, leaving behind them
the quiet lakes and prairies of their northern home, I thought
their voices sounded hoarse and mournful, but this morning
their raucous song was loud and gay. They seemed to be shouting and laughing at one another, and without really knowing it,
my mother and I found ourselves laughing, too, and waving
them on.

My father was coming up the path from the footbridge,
hatless for the first time in months and with his blue-denim
jumper unbuttoned, carrying in each hand a brimming pail of
milk. A wide grin split his winter's beard as he eyed over his
shoulder the eager wingbeats of the oncoming geese behind
him. He staggered a little on the uneven path, slopping milk
lavishly down his pant legs. He seemed not to notice or even
care that morning but came over to join us, and we all stood
and watched the birds with our heads tilted back, slowly turn-

ing on our heels as the geese passed low overhead and vanished in the northern sky. Long after they had disappeared, their clear notes drifted back out of the warm blue haze, announcing to all the ranchers and to our Indian neighbors that spring was here at last.

Every day brought more proof of the beginning of another season: small clumps of dark blue crocuses on furry stems close by a sheltering buckbrush; the prairie suddenly littered with bright pink shooting stars which we called "chickenheads"; on the little knolls pink and blue moss blossoming among the dark green of the ground juniper; *and* the Indians traveling again.

Crazy Dick, the wild young Blackfoot, and some of his riding pals had already picked their way among the dwindling snowbanks and headed for town. Soon the road would dry up and the flooded streams recede enough for the older Indians to travel by in wagons and buckboards. I nearly always saw some of them when we went to Dupuyer—the older men wearing their hair in braids, sitting in the sun on the store porch, half-hidden under high-crowned, broad-brimmed, black felt hats and drab army blankets. The wives and children wandered about the store trying to decide the best buy for their few pennies, much as I did. They were a quiet lot, saying little, the old men talking soundlessly with smooth movements of their hands.

Sometimes I would sneak off to the livery stable to play with Mike, the owner's son. This place was also a magnet for the younger Indians. They would sit on the top rail of the corral fence, looking over the horses penned inside and hoping some local bootlegger would invite them down behind the barn and sell them a pint of whisky, even at twice its worth. None of them seemed to have anything to do—and how I envied them. I always had that doggone empty woodbox waiting beside the stove when I got home, and a thousand other chores, it seemed to me.

One morning my father and my cousin Leo were mending fences on the hillside north of the house—a never-ending ranch chore and especially so after the battering of the winter's storms. Posts had to be replaced or straightened up and reset. The four strands of barbed wire, loose and sagging in places, must be tightened and restapled. I watched them from my vantage place on top of the woodpile behind the house and tried to decide whether to join them or go look for fresh gopher holes in which to set traps. The appearance of an Indian riding over the hill toward my father and cousin decided me. I whistled up our dog, Monday, and started toward them at a fast trot across the flats. I saw the Indian talking for a minute with my father, who then nodded and made a sweeping gesture toward the south and west, where the bulk of our square mile of land lay. Long before I reached them, the Indian rode off along the fence until he came to a place where the wire was down, and there he crossed through and headed toward Scoffin Butte.

A few minutes later I reached the men, short of wind and full of curiosity about the Indian.

"He's looking for winter kills," my father said. "I think there might be one up there behind the ridge. We were short a steer last winter after that sudden blizzard. Remember, Leo?"

Leo nodded. "Yeah. The snow's pretty much melted now, even the drifts, so he might find it."

I knew what winter kills were and that the Indians often looked for them in the early spring. When the cattle were foraging to open range in the winter, occasionally one would stumble into a deep snowbank and flounder there until exhausted, then quickly freeze to death. It would remain hidden in this natural freezer, prefectly preserved, until the melting snows of spring exposed it.

"Can I go and see if he finds it and just watch what he does with it?" I asked my father.

He looked thoughtfully across the valley, then nodded. "Yes. We can keep an eye on you from up here, but don't go over the ridge. And be back to the house by dinner time. You understand?"

Monday and I started off at a steady trot. I always felt safe if Monday was along. He was half as tall as I was and weighed considerably more; he had licked all the dogs and chased away all the coyotes for miles around. Last fall we were after the cows one evening when we started up a coyote napping among the young willows along the creek bank. Before the coyote had been able to get up speed, Monday had run him down and killed him in a short, savage fight. I wasn't positive that he could lick an Indian, but I did feel much braver when he was with me. I panted up the ridge and looked down the far side a hundred feet or so away to where the dismounted Indian was standing beside a dead Hereford steer.

The short, heavyset Blackfoot was surveying his find, now several feet from a shrinking snowdrift, and I wondered if he was considering its possibilities for use in the stew pot. The animal had probably thawed out some time ago, and as I watched, the Indian scraped his foot along its side and then shook his head.

Forgetting my father's warning, I slowly started down the far side of the ridge. The Indian spotted me at once and turned to watch as I drew near. He looked me over carefully, and then raising his hand shoulder high, he said, "How."

I stood tongue-tied.

Finally he asked, "You lost, kid?"

I shook my head and pointed off toward the east, where a smudge of blue smoke rose above the willows and cottonwoods. "I live down there," I said.

He looked solemnly at me and at the smoke for a long moment, then turned back to the carcass.

Like most nine-year-old white kids, I was afraid of Indians. This one seemed friendly enough, though not given to idle talk. I moved a few steps closer and asked, "Is it good to eat?"

He didn't answer, just shook his head.

Reassured by the Indian's easy manner and backed up by Monday's suspicious stare as he sat a few feet behind me, I became bolder. "How can you tell?" I asked.

He stepped over and raked his fingers down the dead steer's side. The hair came off easily, exposing the white skin beneath. "Hair slip. Meat no good," he said gravely.

As I watched, he slit the belly from chin to tail, quickly skinned out the legs and head, and tied his lariat to the neck of the hide. After mounting his pony, he double-half-hitched the rope around the saddlehorn and, holding his horse to a steady pull, ripped the skin free.

Minutes later he had the tightly rolled skin tied in back of the saddle, had washed his hands in the grainy snow and dried them with a few expert passes on the seat of his pants, and had swung up onto his horse. He sat for a few seconds regarding me in friendly silence, then abruptly lifting his hand in a final salute and digging his heels in the pony's flanks, he lunged up the steep side of the hollow. I stood in open-mouthed admiration for his horsemanship as they topped the ridge and turned north, heading for the reservation.

The coyotes had a banquet that night and afterwards sat on the hillside under a full moon and howled. I wondered if they were inviting their friends now that their own bellies were full.

Between the end of the fence-fixing and the start of the spring planting, there were always a few days which my father used for working out his road tax. It was a good time to locate the mudholes and plow out drainage ditches and, if there was time enough and a gravel bank handy, even to dump a few loads of fill where it would do the most good. Directly in front of our house the road crossed the creek on a sturdy wooden bridge. It was a fairly well-traveled highway. Some days as many as two or three rigs passed by and maybe once or twice a year an automobile.

The Indians from the reservation made use of the road a lot. I was accustomed to their passing and knew the names of some of them—Crazy Dick, Chief Salois, who was my father's good friend, and Chief Four Horns, who passed by several times a year and always made a show of it.

After an Indian reached middle age, it seemed to me that he never changed any more, so I couldn't tell much about Chief Four Horns' age except that he dressed like the older Indians. The younger men usually wore the same blue Levis and bright shirts that the white cowboys did, but they never wore the high-heeled cowboy boots, preferring moccasins or low-heeled shoes. They were very proud of their horses and often went by in small bands, riding at a fast gallop and staring straight ahead, ignoring us completely. However, after a day in town and a few shots of bootleg whisky, they would return late at night, racing down the lane, hooting and yelling, their horses' hoofs drumming on the hard-packed road and hammering across the bridge planks. The racket receded as they climbed the hill beyond the house and suddenly ceased when they left the road and struck across the thick buffalo grass of the northern rangeland. This always scared the daylights out of my mother and sisters, and the teacher, and me too, though I hated to admit it. I did enjoy the excitement, though, and often wished desperately that I, too, had been born an Indian and was free to ride the prairies and do as I pleased. Chief Four Horns passed by in a more restrained manner, but his proud bearing and fancy rig always managed to put a bit of sparkle in an otherwise drab day.

One bright clear morning in early June I was sitting on our footbridge with my younger sister, Lucy. Fed by the recent heavy rains and the fast melting snow of the high Rockies, Sheep Creek was running bank-full. Our footbridge at that time was simply two large pine logs laid closely together and reaching from bank to bank, just comfortably clear of the water. We were having a wonderful time playing our favorite game, "flying." We sat side by side, facing upstream, our bare feet a scant inch above the flood, and looked straight down into the racing current. At first the water just swirled by, brown and flecked with creamy foam. Then something would click in my head, the water stopped dead, and my sister and I in our imaginary log air-ship were flying upsteam at a dazzling speed, swooping and swerving, the wind strong in our faces and the water roaring in our ears.

During one of our most exciting runs, I became aware of clinking steel-rimmed wheels and pounding unshod hooves on the road. I swiveled my eyes from the water to the nearby hillside and stopped my flying with a breathtaking jerk. When I saw it was the chief coming, I raised my feet and swung around on the logs to get a good look as he rolled by.

I always supposed Chief Four Horns was a very rich and powerful man because he rode in a shiny black topless buggy with bright yellow wheels and drove the most beautiful pair of matched sorrel ponies I had ever seen. He sat soldier-straight on the seat, his high-crowned black felt hat dead-square on his head and his two long braids of jet-black hair floating behind his shoulders. The buggy whip was perpendicular in his right hand, the reins taut in his left, and his eyes focused straight ahead. But he always seemed to see everything that was going on around the ranch as he passed.

That morning my father had tied Snort to the corral fence and was currying off the last of his matted winter coat, leaving him a glossy dark-red. The chief spotted them and swerved to a stop along the lane fence nearby. We watched as my father left off his grooming and walked over for a talk with him. After a few minutes of quiet conversation, the chief raised his whip in salute, then swung back into the road and off toward town.

My sister and I immediately ran over to the fence to stand beside my father and watch the disappearing buggy, hoping he would tell us what Chief Four Horns had said. He paid no attention to us, however. Lucy, after fidgeting for a few minutes, couldn't hold back her curiosity and blurted out, "What did the chief want, Pa?"

"We talked business," he answered absently.

Lucy was six, curious, and inclined to be fresh. "What kind of business you got with that old Indian?" she asked in her most impudent tone.

My father usually laughed at her spunk and independence, but he frowned on this kind of forwardness. Deciding she needed a lesson, he answered in his offhand way, "He wants to trade me that pair of sorrel mares for you. I told him I'd think about it and let him know later."

Lucy's jaw dropped, and she stared unbelieving at her father, who stood looking thoughtfully after his departing visitor. Finally she got her voice back. "Mama won't let you do no such of a thing." she shouted defiantly and bolted off to the safety of the house.

My father chuckled as he watched her running up the path, then remarked to me in a confidential way, "That ought to hold her for a while."

And it did hold her—for a while. But in a couple of weeks she was back to her old ways. One morning she was so sassy at the breakfast table that my father could stand it no longer. "Lucy!" he said sternly. "The very next time the chief comes by, he can have you, and I'll have a nice team of horses. I hope he can teach you some manners because I sure can't!" We all laughed except Lucy and my mother, who frowned at him and shook her head.

During the spring rains a good-sized pond formed in the swale just across the road in front of our house. I sailed on it on a very unseaworthy raft built of fenceposts held together with slats and ten-penny nails. The water was shallow, and I risked only a ducking if I fell overboard, but the little kids were absolutely forbidden to go near the thing. Lucy was a borderline case, though, and I occasionally flirted with trouble from my mother by coaxing her to go sailing with me.

Shortly after finishing breakfast one morning, Lucy and I were floating a dozen feet from shore when we noticed a rig coming down the hill. Sure enough, it was the chief driving his frisky sorrels. My father, standing by the bunkhouse, waved to him as he came up. The chief responded by swinging the horses neatly through the open gate, coming to an abrupt halt in the midst of a rising cloud of dust.

"It's Old Four Horns," I said. "And I bet I know what *he* wants."

Lucy's normally tanned and freckled face paled swiftly under the layer of mud it had collected in the past hour, and she turned desperate eyes on me.

"I think that's an Indian suitcase," I added slyly, pointing to a large woven-willow basket now clearly visible in the back of the buggy.

She was on her feet in a flash and without hesitation made a flying leap from the raft toward the house. I was too scared to move and expected her to disappear under the water like a stone. It was barely waist deep for her, though, and she churned it into a froth as she made for the nearby shore. It took all her energy and breath to reach dry land and scramble up the slippery bank. But when she reached the road, she made up for lost time and began screaming frantically for her mother as she raced for the house. I was close behind by the time she had clambered through the fence, leaving a long strip of gingham from her dress fluttering from a sharp barb. My father interrupted

his conversation with Chief Four Horns to stare at our wild approach, then, thoroughly frightened, excused himself and hurried across the bridge to intercept us. About the same time the
kitchen door banged open, and Iris, closely followed by our
mother, dashed out, and we all met in a confused huddle in the
front yard.

Lucy made a flying leap for her mother and locked her
arms around her neck, shutting off her wind and allowing only
some strangling noises to issue from my mother's throat.

My father stared at Lucy's soaked clothes, her torn dress,
and a long scratch down one leg, then reached out and got a
good hold on my long hair.

"What happened to her?" he asked me grimly. He knew
from past experience that when something like this happened, I
usually had a hand in it. I saw a licking coming up, so I answered in a hurry, "She thinks you sold her to Chief Four
Horns and that he has come to get her."

That really jolted him. He goggled at me, then let go of my
hair and began to make soothing motions with his hands toward
my mother. She managed to break Lucy's stranglehold by sheer
muscle power, took a deep breath, and turned fiercely on him.
"Damn it all, Ed. I've told you a million times about scaring the
kids! Now look what you've done!"

He stammered, "Gosh, Peg, I'm sorry. I didn't think—"

"That's the trouble with you. You never think," my
mother yelled, breaking in with one of her usual sweeping state-
ments. She stared across the creek at the innocent old chief, who
sat waiting patiently for my father's return, and continued hys-
terically, "I could shoot both you and that old Indian right
now." And gathering her wildly sobbing child to her breast, she
stalked off to the house, occasionally glaring back over her
shoulder in our direction.

My father looked thoroughly beaten and was attempting a
sickly smile when there was a splintering crash over by the
bunkhouse. Chief Four Horns had been sitting in his buggy,
waiting for all the foolish excitement to subside, but he must
have had sharp ears, for when my mother screamed something
about Indians and shooting, he went into action. Hauling back

on the lines, he put the excited sorrels into a fast reverse turn. That's when the wagon hit my mother's rose trellis. (Her father, a landscape gardener in Helena, often sent vines and shrubs to beautify our bare prairie ranch. When his half-dozen rambler rose bushes had arrived early in the spring, my mother immediately hounded my father into planting them down by the bunkhouse and also into building a beautiful trellis for them to climb on.) By the time the buggy stopped, there wasn't much of the trellis still standing, and the chief was really scared. After straightening out the horses and heading them toward the gate, Chief Four Horns applied his whip briskly to their backsides. Hanging grimly to the reins, his hat for once over one ear, he took the turn on two wheels and disappeared down the lane behind a funnel of dust.

It took some time, but eventually my mother could laugh about Lucy and the chief and even about the mangled trellis, but never again did my father talk about trading any of us kids off—especially to the Indians.

From this experience and others like it, it is easy to understand why my mother could never accept my father's free and easy relationship with the Blackfeet, nor approve my admiration for what I thought was their wonderful way of life. Of all our Indian neighbors there was only one family, the Salois, that she looked upon without fear and suspicion.

At least once every year Chief Salois and his large family would come by on their hunting and berrying trips. They traveled in a couple of Studebaker lumber wagons covered with canvas stretched over wooden hoops, something like the early prairie schooners, and gathered the ripening chokecherries from along the stream banks and the purple service berries growing on hillside bushes. They were friendly and quiet and well liked by the ranchers. Sometimes they camped on our place, and this was always a treat for me.

One cool night in late August I walked with my father down the road a short distance and out into the freshly cut meadow to where they were camped by the creek. The small fire, still glowing between the fireplace stones, looked very inviting in the chill dusk. The old chief and two younger men sat cross-legged close to its friendly warmth, but there was no sign of the women and children. I guessed they must be asleep in the wagons. All three Indians offered a grave "How," and my father answered with his usual hearty "Howdy." I was rather awed by their severe and dignified expressions, and said nothing, just sidled up to the fire and found a seat on the ground beside my father.

It was some time before anything more was said. Finally my father asked if they were going berrying, and they all looked at him and nodded in unison, then went back to staring at the fire.

At last Chief Salois commented, "Saw bear track yesterday. Up at head of Sheep Creek."

I straightened up with a shiver of excitement. Wow! A bear! I peered through the gloom up our valley to where it disappeared under the flank of Split Mountain. All was quiet and peaceful, but then everyone knew that bears didn't make much noise traveling around and were hard to see after dark.

"Grizzly?" my father asked.

The chief nodded. "Big one. We look for berries somewhere else now." After a short pause he went on. "We don't bother grizzly bear. He very dangerous. Look !"

He slipped off his heavy wool shirt, baring his upper body. The left arm was badly crippled with the muscles shrunken and deformed, and his chest was criss-crossed with long, ragged scars. He told us in his slow quiet way how as a young man he had followed a wounded grizzly, and because he was in a hurry and careless, the bear had outsmarted him and ambushed him and run him down. As he lay on his back under the bear, he had worked his left arm up and shoved his elbow into the bear's mouth as it fought to reach his throat. Somehow he had managed to draw his hunting knife with his right hand and stab blindly into the huge body above him. By good luck he drove the heavy knife between the bear's ribs and deep into its heart.

His hunting companions found him later and brought him back to camp more dead than alive. It was many months before he recovered and could hunt again. "Ever since then," the chief concluded, "I keep away from grizzly bear."

The other two Indians nodded in agreement, and my father observed that that was the smart thing to do. "Hope he stays up there and don't come down here and bother the stock," he added.

"He won't. Lots of berries up there this year," one of the younger Indians said. "He likes them better than meat." And then went on with a faint grin, "Besides he don't like people any more than people like him. He smart!"

Conversation again came to a halt, and we all relaxed into a companionable silence. Several minutes later my father asked if they had seen any of his stock when they crossed the northern range.

Chief Salois said he had noticed quite a few along Birch Creek. Birch Creek was the southern boundary of the Blackfoot reservation, and it was a well-known fact that sometimes a fat beef steer disappeared if he wandered across it.

Then he continued soberly, "Shorthorn steer almost as good eating as buffalo."

My father laughed and said he guessed he'd better have a look.

All this talk apparently exhausted the Indians, and they seemed to have nothing more to say. A few minutes later we said goodnight and started for the house. I had to stretch my legs pretty hard to keep up with my father that night, but I had a healthy fear of bears. You can bet that after hearing the chief's story and knowing that there *was* a bear hanging around—and a big one at that—I wasn't going to get left behind.

Still, I couldn't help wishing I was one of those free and easy Indian kids sleeping in the wagon. The fall before, I had gone camping with my cousins and the hired man on a firewood-cutting expedition far up in the foothills. Even though I was almost brained with a falling tree and one night nearly died of fright because I was sure a grizzly bear was chasing me down a game trail, my enthusiasm for camping was in no way dampened. My mother was a darned good cook, but her baked potatoes never tasted as good as that last little bit of potato that's left unburned when it is roasted in a roaring campfire. And those delicious steaks she fried in a big iron skillet didn't really compare with one charred black on both sides from a pitch-pine open fire, left bloody-raw on the inside, and eaten with lots of salt and greasy fingers. I didn't have to undress at night, either, just pulled off my shoes and crawled under the blankets and woke up in the chilly dawn, long before sunrise, to the crackle of a freshly built campfire and the smell of boiling coffee. How I wished I was one of the Salois grandchildren and was spending the whole summer camping out.

In spite of his nonchalance while talking with the Indians, my father was worried about his wandering livestock. A prime western steer selling at eight cents a pound on the hoof was worth about seventy-five dollars, and that was a lot of money. So he left right after breakfast the next morning and teamed up with Carl Embody, a nearby rancher, to round up all the loose stock near the reservation and drive them back to our side of the range.

When he came back that evening and walked up the path to the kitchen door, my mother was watching him through the window. "Your father has been up to something." she remarked to me. "I haven't seen him look so pleased with himself in months."

In spite of all our coaxing, he wouldn't tell us about his trip until he had eaten and polished off the dessert, apple pie and whipped cream. He prolonged the suspense further by getting his huge calabash pipe down from the shelf and loading it with a charge of powerful T & B tobacco. When the pipe was drawing to his satisfaction, he looked around, snickered to himself a couple of times, and began talking slowly between puffs.

"We had a lot of territory to cover, and the going was rough among those draws leading down to Birch Creek and through the undergrowth along the streams. We didn't see much stock, either, and by noon we were hot, hungry, and discouraged. About that time we broke out on the bank of Birch Creek across from a small natural meadow. On one side of this hayfield was the biggest cottonwood tree I ever saw, with a log cabin standing in its shade. An Indian sat with his back to a tree, smoking a corncob pipe, and all the time the horses were drinking, Carl kept looking at him. Finally, he asked me if I didn't think it was Buffalo Tail."

My father interrupted himself by turning to Leo and asking, "You remember him, don't you—the one Sam Harris thinks is a smart-alec?"

Leo agreed. "Yeah! He's pulled a couple of dandy jokes on the Harris brothers, or so I've heard."

"Well," my father continued, "I wasn't sure. You know how all Indians look pretty much alike to me. Anyway, we decided to ride over and ask if he's seen any cattle around. When we got over there, he stood up and said 'How,' and Carl asked him if he was Buffalo Tail. He nodded, and I asked him if he had seen any of my **U** stock around [**U** was my father's brand], and he said 'Ugh' which I took to mean 'yes.' So I asked him where. He pointed off to the other side of the creek and waved his arm in a way that took in at least half of Teton County. 'Over there. No cows this side of creek,' he said. We sat on our horses for a minute, trying to decide whether he was lying or not, when he suddenly asked us to stay for dinner. We were leary about eating with him because we had heard that the Indian housekeeping wasn't so hot and you know how squeamish Carl is.

"Everything looked fine outside, and as much as we could see of the kitchen through the open door seemed neat and clean; and besides, Buffalo Tail acted so friendly, we didn't want to hurt his feelings. So we agreed, and he went inside to see if dinner was ready. Carl kept shaking his head and saying we were a couple damn fools to stay. I told him to hell with his worries, and I was hungry enough to eat anything any Indian could dish up right now. The Blackfoot came to the door in a few minutes and waved us in. The kitchen was slick as a whistle and so was Mrs. Buffalo Tail, who was cooking some kind of a stew over the fire."

Here was something I had wondered about so I interrupted his story to ask if she cooked on a fire in the middle of the floor like they do in their teepees. My father laughed and shook his head, "Of course not, dummy; she's got a stove just like ours.

And boy, did that stew smell good!

"Well, once we started eating, even Carl forgot his suspicions and enjoyed it. When the plates were cleaned up, we sat back and relaxed, and Carl pulled out the makings and started rolling a cigarette. He looked across the table at the Indian and grinned. 'That was mighty fine meat in that pot.' he said. 'What was it? Beef or venison?' Buffalo Tail never batted an eyelash. 'That was dog,' he said."

My father paused and looked around, and we all laughed.

"I'll have to admit," he went on, "that my stomach took a flip-flop, and I felt like a damn fool, but it was worth it to see Carl's face. He dropped the cigarette, grabbed his mouth with both hands, and started for the door on a run, and he made it too. When I looked at Buffalo Tail again, he had a beautiful smile on his face, and I knew I had to come up with something good. Without really thinking, I just opened my mouth and said, 'You know, Buffalo Tail! That was the best damn dog meat I ever ate.' "

We all howled with laughter, and my father sat back in his armchair with a wide, self-satisfied smile on his face. It gradually faded and was replaced with a deep frown as he stared at his empty plate. Finally, sensing that we were all watching him, he looked up at my mother and said in a voice of grudging admiration for the Indian. "Do you suppose that that damn redskin really fed us dog? Or was it one of my best steers?"

My father never did find out the answer to his question, and I never fully satisfied my curiosity as to what the Indians really ate, what kind of houses they lived in, whether the kids regularly went to school, and whether their mothers and fathers always found chores for them to do as mine did.

One day I was returning home from the Howes', to whom my mother occasionally "lent" one of us kids for a night since they were childless, when Chief Salois, driving his big camping wagon, overtook me and offered me a lift. As I climbed up over the wheel, an old woman and a couple of young children retreated into the back of the wagon under the canvas, leaving the wide spring seat for the chief and me. I got a quick peek through the opening and saw them sitting in a row, leaning against the wagon box. I sat up real straight beside the chief because I knew they were all staring with unblinking eyes at my back and listening to every breath I took. The old Indian wasn't much of a talker at first, and everything was quiet except for the rattling and squeaking of the wagon, the jingling of the trace chains, and the occasional running snort of a tired horse.

I was getting kind of desperate for something to say to break the quiet when we started to bump across a wide series of deep ruts, half hidden under the long range grass. Once I had asked my father what this road was, but he didn't know. The chief had always lived here. I thought maybe he might know about it, so I asked him, "Where does that road go?"

He shook his head. "That's no road," he said. "That's the old Indian Trail."

"But it looks like a road. They didn't have wagons, did they?"

"No wagons," he said. "Just Indian feet! Indian horses! Indian travois!"

I looked along the many rows of deep ruts we were still crossing and felt pretty sure he was wrong. "But it would take a million Indians a thousand years to do that," I protested.

Again he nodded. "That's right. Our old men tell us that way back when the land was covered with ice, the Indians, thick like the geese in spring and fall, started following this trail each year. They came from back there [he waved vaguely toward the north] and went off that way [pointing south] until they came to the land where there is no prairie, only sand and mountains and rivers deep, deep, in the ground."

We had known Chief Salois for many years and had respect for his words, but this seemed a mighty tall story to me, and I must have looked it, for he said, "Wait. I'll show you."

He turned the team west, and we followed along the side of the rutted trail a mile or so until we came to the brow of a hill that overlooked our valley and the miles of prairie and beyond. Here he pulled the horses to a halt and pointed down to the ground. "See! Indian ring!" he said. "Here they camped along the Great North Trail."

Laid out on the ground nearby was a perfect ten-foot circle

of large cobblestones with a small heap of fire-blackened rocks in its center. Close by was another ring. We got down and walked along until I had counted a dozen or more.

"This is where the Indian pitched his wigwam long ago. Here he watched for his enemies. He could see where the buffalo and antelope were thickest and easiest to hunt. When he went away, he left the stones that held his teepee down and marked his campfire. We call them the 'Old Indian' rings."

Funny, I had never noticed these rings before. I couldn't even remember hearing talk about them. Maybe white people didn't see lots of things that the Indians did.

We stood and stared off at the mighty mountains half hidden in the afternoon haze. There was a faint smell of smoke in the air—probably a forest fire over in the Flathead Valley, I thought.

"Do the Blackfeet ever follow the North Trail anymore?" I asked.

"No," he said. "But my father, and his father, and his father's father used to follow the buffalo which went south along it every fall as far as the Deerlodge Valley, where the high mountains protected them from the cold winds. The hunting was good there all winter. When spring came and the air was warm again and the buffalo grass thick and green, they came back up the old trail to the wide prairie and the shining mountains. It's not like that anymore. Indians now must live on reservations."

I looked out across the miles and miles of mountain and prairie, purple and gold under the late summer sun, where once the Blackfeet had hunted and camped, where they had lived and died. I saw now a few lonely ranches along the streambeds and scattered bands of cattle feeding on the rich rangegrass— white man's land, our land. For a moment I almost forgot the proud old Indian with the sad voice and the wistful eyes, and all that he had told me. I was watching a long-billed curlew settle into the prairiegrass with fluttering wings, his plaintive *curlée, curlée* dying away to silence when he reached the ground.

The text for this book was set in Baskerville
by George Banta Company, Menasha, Wisconsin,
who also did the printing and binding. The
paper is Hilding Hi-Bulk, cream white,
and the cloth is Columbia Mill's Renne,
natural finish.

Design by John Beyer